THE LAST
THUNK

A Novel

Gerard Farrell

four

THE LAST THUNK

A Novel

Gerard Farrell

GREENPOINT PRESS
NEW YORK, NY

THE LAST THUNK by Gerard Farrell
www.ggfarrell.com

ISBN 978-0-9906194-7-5

Library of Congress Cataloging-in-Publication Data

Book Designer: Robert L. Lascaro
LascaroDesign.com

Greenpoint Press
A division of New York Writers Resources
greenpointpress.org
200 Riverside Boulevard, Suite 32E
New York, NY 10069

New York Writers Resources:
· newyorkwritersresources.com
· newyorkwritersworkshop.com
· greenpointpress.org
· prisonwrites.org

Printed in the United States
on acid-free paper

To Maricel. For everything.

CONTENTS

PART II: 2007-2008

The Ten of Swords

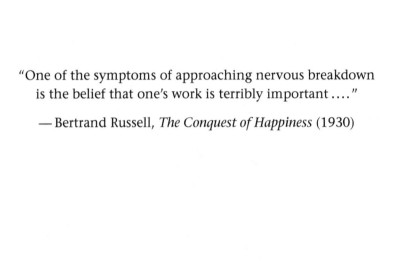

"One of the symptoms of approaching nervous breakdown is the belief that one's work is terribly important ...."

— Bertrand Russell, *The Conquest of Happiness* (1930)

PART I: 2002-2007
You'll need to be sober for this.

CHAPTER ONE

World Begins
(2007)

I SHOULD HAVE BEEN SATISFIED with Carlyle Nash Media's 2007 holiday schedule: 11 closed-shop days in addition to my four weeks of vacation. But five years with the company had spoiled me.

"Don't we usually get Columbus Day?," I muttered as I ran my finger down the gilded, die-cut calendar. My first impulse was to check last year's schedule, but that would have to wait. I'd just been summoned for a 9:00 AM with Mitch.

Mitch Blake, that is. My boss. He wasn't a fan of the holiday calendar either. But for different reasons. The office was to Mitch what a spa or a pub is to a human. It was the place he wanted to be over any other. And he seemed surprised when people felt differently. If you asked Mitch to approve you for a long weekend, you'd get the same question each time.

"Oh. Weren't you just on vacation?" he'd say while paging back through his leather-bound planner.

"Ummm, no Mitch. It's actually been a while. There was the oral surgery last year, and that one day in February when my cat—"

"Fine. Just make sure I can reach you."

But Mitch—star publisher with a string of ad-sales resurrections at magazines such as *True Gent, Fine Estates*, and *Bellwether* to his name—had recently begun to see the value of a day off. Not for himself, but for the overburdened staff of his latest project, Carlyle Nash's most important launch ever: *World* Magazine.

Nearly two years in the making, *World* was to be a general-interest title so wide in scope that we had budget for embedded war reporters in the Horn of Africa, dueling beat writers in Silicon Valley, and even a Royal Family correspondent. On the ad side, our sales reps could expense everything from three-hour client lunches at Per Se to charter jet rentals. When Alec Baldwin narrated our 90-second promotional video, he told the director, "I haven't been paid this much since *The Hunt for Red October*."

Salaries were generous too, but in the heat of the pre-launch stage, we on the business staff would have gladly traded them for a day off. Everyone had been pushed hard. What had once been a place of pleasant hallway greetings was becoming one of passing eye rolls that screamed, "Can you believe this shit?"

So with eight weeks to go before the ad deadline for May's premiere issue, Mitch dangled a carrot: if we could bring in 30 more ad pages, to shatter the Carlyle Nash single-issue record of 189, everyone would get the day off on the Tuesday after Memorial Day. Mitch had at long last taken the pulse of the office and now knew what we needed to hear: *four-day weekend*. Our sales staff responded.

Jim Keane closed a four-page Mercedes unit within a day of the announcement. The Chicago office locked down an eight-page advertorial from Dow Chemical. Detroit delivered Ford F-150 and Skoal. Fist bumps made a return.

In four short weeks, the *World* premiere issue hit its 190 ad-page goal. Equally jammed with editorial features on everyone and everything from Lance Armstrong to Lehman Brothers, biowarfare to Beyoncé, the inch-thick debut would make that sweet *thunk* when dropped on a table. To Mitch, it was a sound as beautiful as his children's laughter. Most important, he had his record—delivering on his promise to Calvin Moreland, Carlyle Nash's octogenarian chairman, to set a new bar.

When I took my seat in front of Mitch's desk, which was handcrafted from ebony and Carpathian Elm, he was on the first of his 30 morning phone calls. As usual, it was to the *New York Tribune's* Lou Lamont, the most influential media columnist in Manhattan. Mitch, a PR virtuoso, had already succeeded in making *World* the most talked-about, anticipated launch ever. With more than a few competitors hoping to see us fail, spreading the news that the premiere issue was *too full to accept more ads* had to be equal parts imperative and intoxicating.

"Lou Lamont...how are you, my friend?"

As he spoke—phone between ear and shoulder—I watched him simultaneously tap out emails and cross items off a to-do list. Unlike most other publishers at Carlyle Nash, who rose to the top of a magazine masthead on raw ambition, Mitch had gotten there on brains, organizational skills, and consummate attention to detail. That he could pass for a champion surfer was the bow on an envy-inducing package. He was six-foot-two, blue-eyed, with close-cropped blond hair, and at the age of 46 he was in the best shape of his life. His wife, Danica, was an inarguable 10—blond too. His adorable pre-teen daughters, blond. If you stared long enough at the sun-splashed family photos on his desk, you'd be transported to Greenwich. Behind him, on a spacious windowsill, sat shots of him with Jon Stewart, Jack Welch, Muhammad Ali, and Katie Couric. Fencing equipment lay in a corner.

"I'm not worried about *The Globalist*," said Mitch. "Evans and that tired old pamphlet can say whatever they want about *World*. They're scared of us, Lou. Don't quote me on that, though. Let me just say..."

He covered the phone.

"What's *The Globalist's* median age on the affluent survey?"

"Fifty-five point four," I answered.

"Median age of fifty-five, Lou. Declining household income too. That's *The Globalist's* readership—old, white, and eating out of cans. There's your quote."

As Mitch moved on to *World's* long-term business model, I congratulated myself for knowing the median age off the top of my head. *Be ready*, I had exhorted myself during the walk down the hallway. *Focus.* But with one right answer, I began to relax a bit.

Good job. Way to be prepared. And Mitch knows it. How could he not? He knows. He hired you. And when do you not deliver? You're doing great. No one can do this job like you. But what is he writing on his pad? Looks like my name. Wait, no, that's not my name. It's someone else's name. Whose? Someone he wants to interview? Why? For a job? What job? Stop it. What the fuck is wrong with you? You're fine. You're good.

As I took a long sip of bottled water, Mitch moved on to the standard closing: 30 seconds on Lou's golf game and 30 on his kids. He tossed a worn pencil in the trash, picked out a freshly sharpened one, and crossed *Lamont* off his list. He flashed me the usual thumbs-up without raising his head. I was free to go.

"You look tired," said Mitch's assistant, Naomi, as I passed her desk.

"That's because I am."

And I was. My name is Paul Cavanaugh. I served as the marketing director on what many call the industry's last big launch. To say that *World* changed me for a while would be an understatement. The ill-fated magazine took a lot out of me and a lot away from me.

But I still have something Mitch doesn't.

* * * *

THE BEACH BALL ARRIVED in my in-box about a month later, not long after the May issue officially launched—on the day Diane left for a Puerto Rico vacation.

"You're killing us, Paul," she said as the airport car idled in the driveway that morning.

I glanced at my watch and saw that there was ample time before the flight, yet she hadn't dried her hair. Her damp auburn ringlets filled the foyer with the scent of Pantene as I bent to pick up her stuffed weekend bag.

"I got it," she said as she snatched it and hoisted it over her narrow shoulders. She added something about a new lawn service on her way out, but I missed it. I wasn't listening too closely. I didn't dare ask her to repeat herself because she'd been saying for weeks that I didn't listen to anyone or anything but my own thoughts and "Lord Mitch."

While it was true that *World* and other distractions abounded, I mostly clung to my position that the real marital drag was Diane's unwillingness to consider the historical significance of the magazine. Perhaps a week in the tropics would help her see my side of things. I had unsuccessfully tried to outline my position again the night before, after stumbling in from *World*'s premiere party—or, by Diane's count, *World*'s sixth premiere party.

She did have a point. Carlyle Nash's standard operating procedure for a new magazine was to debut in May but wait until September to commence monthly frequency. In the interim, public and industry reaction to the premiere were gauged via deep market research by day and extensive social interaction at night. In other words, we listened for *World*, we talked about *World*, and we drank to *World*.

She'd been waiting up, sipping tea and watching TV with the sound turned off, when I got home at two in the morning. As soon as I came in the door, she switched off the television and took her cup into the kitchen. I followed, making my case.

"I had to be there, Diane. The first year is critical."

"Where is your jacket, Paul? How many drinks did you have tonight?"

"You're shouting. Don't wake the baby."

"You're shouting. You idiot."

"I'm so hungry."

The arguments had almost become routine. On we would go, until I passed out on the couch to the oddly comforting whir of Diane's electric breast pump—punctuated by her occasional sigh or "Ouch." A few hours of sleep later, I'd be off to the Cold Spring Harbor train station after a kiss on her head, a mumbled apology, and a peek into Aidan's crib—marveling that he had become a toddler so soon.

What had made the previous night's bout different was the shove Diane had given me on her way out of the kitchen. Hard. Intentional. I stumbled backward, knocking a tea kettle to the floor and saw Diane's tears of frustration as she bent to pick it up.

"It's come to this," she said. "I'm beating you."

Yet I still told myself that every couple goes through rough patches. Every man has a year of selfish choices. And if in fact my diversions, vices, and misplaced priorities were the chief causes of our problems, I vowed they'd only be temporary. I watched Diane get in the airport limo and shut the door. She didn't wave. We didn't kiss goodbye.

Her flight left at 6:00 AM, and I had to get ready for work, so my mother arrived early to watch Aidan. As usual, she told me I looked tired—Irish code for "I see you've been drinking"—and that my father had also started "filling out" in his thirties. She added that commuting had stolen decades from his life. I nodded absently in agreement, kissed her goodbye in mid-sentence, and hustled off to catch my own diesel hearse to Manhattan.

"You've got to get rid of that car, Paul," she said as I crossed the lawn.

"Never, Old Woman. I want to be buried in this thing."

My battered station car was a rust-encrusted 1975 Chevy Malibu that my neo-affluent neighbors wanted condemned. I warmed it up for a few minutes before pulling away from the curb. As my mother waved from the doorway—looking a bit more stooped than usual—my thoughts turned to my father.

He had bought the used car for me when I graduated high school. I was hopelessly attached to it. Each time I made the heavy two-handed turn onto West Neck Road, I could hear him saying how power steering was completely unnecessary in a vehicle. The memory had always made me chuckle, but of late was making me well up. As I pulled into the station parking lot, I jammed the gearshift up into Park and rubbed my temples.

Would you stop with the fucking crying? What is this? Go to work.

* * * *

I ARRIVED EARLIER THAN USUAL at my office in the Carlyle Nash building, a gleaming Times Square tower, on that warm and sunny Friday. As odd a sight as the beach ball was sitting in my in-box, my first order of business was the usual. I slid open my desk drawer, reached for the Duane Reade aspirin bottle, and popped three. Good for the heart, I told myself.

I picked up the beach ball. It was a miniature one—roughly the size of a grapefruit, with alternating yellow and hot pink bands. Tied to the air spout was an elegantly designed card that read:

SUMMER STAFF INCENTIVE
*Drive 150 Ad Pages into the September Issue
and Everyone Gets a Free Day Off
around Labor Day Weekend!*

"Wow," I whispered. "He's going to the well again."

For a second issue, 150 ad pages was an ambitious goal. Clearly, Mitch was emboldened by the success of the Memorial Day incentive. But did he really have to use this ploy again? The premiere issue had only just hit newsstands and we still had a fair amount of lead time to the July deadline for September ads. Plus, we were supposedly better than halfway there from what I had seen in the estimates.

"We'll see," I said as I untied the card and pinned it to my cluttered bulletin board, giving an extra push to get the pin through the ridiculously thick paper stock. Our promotion department seemed determined to blow through our $125 million launch budget on glossy internal communications alone. As for the beach ball, I figured I would take that home to Aidan—maybe try to spend some time with him over the weekend, check in on his motor skills.

As I set the beach ball down next to my favorite photo of me and Diane—her, pregnant, pretty, happier; me smiling, relaxed—Thad Bellows, our noxious National Sales Director, strode in with a passing knock on my open door. Thad had a habit of never sitting down in one of the two chairs opposite my desk. Instead he would perch himself on the elevated bench-like window sill behind me, so that I would have to swing my chair around to look up at him. He did it to remind me of rank, of course. Or maybe he just liked the way the sun lit up his highlights and Tiffany cufflinks.

"Did you get my email last night?" he asked.

"I didn't, Thad. My Blackberry was down."

"You should get that checked. Mine never goes down."

"That doesn't surprise me. What's up?"

"I've been asking you for a competitive presentation on *The Globalist*'s weaknesses for more than a month. What's the status?"

The truthful answer to that question was, "It's nowhere, because Mitch didn't ask me for it—you did," but I instead told him to put me on the agenda for the following Wednesday's sales meeting. I would be ready to share something with the staff then.

"Good," he said. "You'll be first up."

"I'm counting the days."

You couldn't fend off Thad forever and I didn't need him sending Mitch an email about how I was being uncooperative. You never wanted to be the guy who directly or indirectly caused Mitch to waste his time refereeing a pissing match. And telling Thad I'd be ready Wednesday was also a way for me to set a deadline for myself. I never missed them and I thrived on quick turnaround—the main reasons Mitch had put me in the job.

Satisfied for now, Thad gave one last disgusted up-and-down to my buy-one-get-two-free suit. He leaned forward a few inches and looked me in the eyes.

"There are creams for dark circles, you know."

"Thanks for caring, Thad."

He glided out before I could ask his thoughts on the beach ball. I was actually curious. But he was already next door in my friend Paige's office, bitching about some merchandising mix-up.

Most people at *World* wondered why Mitch had even hired Thad, much less made him his Number Two. Mitch was direct, but rarely confrontational. There was a folded-hands serenity about him when dealing with staff. If you had the answers he needed, interactions were short and smooth. If you didn't, he would calmly tell you he needed them right away, but would almost always advise the best way to go about tracking down those very answers. However, if he had to do too much of the latter, you were thrown into the ring with Thad. He was the overtly aggressive yin to Mitch's unimpeachably professional yang. The muscle. A graceless wretch like Thad was necessary to keep back-office people and second-stringers jumping, but also to preserve Mitch's reputation as a good and benevolent leader. If you walked away from the job—or were walked away from the job—it had nothing to do with Mitch. Executives could go from a corner office to selling hot nuts on Seventh Avenue and they would still say that working for Mitch was the greatest thing that ever happened to them. At least that's the way I saw it. Mitch was mystifying to many, but on my best days I was convinced I had him figured out. On my worst days, I'd waste hours second-guessing myself. Either way, studying his methods and discerning his motives had become a hobby of sorts. Diane called it an obsession. The more I unlocked, and the more I thought I could see what others didn't, the more I respected him. He was a tactical genius. And he had hired me.

Don't even think about Thad. You're good with Mitch.

I heard Paige screaming, "That's bullshit, Thad!" as he exited her office, so I scrambled over to shut my door before she could come in to vent. Paige was head of Promotions. I had always been a good listener and friend to her, but *World*'s frenetic pace was increasingly producing in me a feigned compassion. I felt a bit guilty about it, but I just didn't have the time to mock-earnestly listen to her complaints today.

I was sitting down to work on the presentation when the phone rang. *Extension 6216. Blake, Mitchell.* I took a deep breath.

"Hi, Mitch."

I could hear him tapping out an email.

"Paul. *Currents.* Could you let me know their reader-per-copy…when you have a minute?"

"Three-point-eight-nine."

"Three-point-eight-nine… Someone had his coffee today."

"I did, Mitch. On the train. There's a Seven-Eleven right near my station."

Wait, was that a joke? Shit, too late.

I could hear him shuffling papers, continuing to multitask. I wasn't sure if I was supposed to hang up first.

"Did you get your beach ball?" he asked.

"Yes. I think it's great, Mitch. And thanks too. I'm sure we'll hit that number, right?"

"We'll see. Have to go to an eight-fifteen."

"Hey Mitch, I did have a quick question about—"

He hung up.

I held the receiver for a few seconds as I stared straight ahead. Conversations with Mitch were never very long, but this was clearly a brush-off.

Maybe he didn't like the circulation memo I wrote yesterday. Did I botch it? Was it off-message? Why else would he just ignore my question and hang up? Shit, maybe he doesn't even really have an eight-fifteen. I could ask Naomi, but she's probably not in yet.

I stood over my keyboard and hit command-P. The color printers were just across from Mitch's office. By standing at one, you could get a quick view to see if he was in or out—an old trick I used when looking to leave for Happy Hour. My office—the biggest and best I had ever had, with a large window and great view—was on the opposite end of the floor. I hustled out and down the hall.

Printer Number One was conveniently jammed, so I lingered over its control panel and muttered dramatically. The time read 8:19 AM. Mitch was still in his office.

Maybe he did brush me off. No. Stop it. You're being ridiculous, you fucking asshole.

Mitch strode out, Blackberry and planner in hand.

"That thing still messed up?" he asked as he passed. "Just call a tech guy, Paul. You don't need to be doing that. Hey, leave me two more copies of the circulation memo. It was fine. No changes."

"Thanks, Mitch," I shouted after him. "Thank you, Mitch."

I instantly felt like a moron for thanking him twice. And it didn't help that Naomi was in, and had been watching the whole thing.

"Hey, Paul. Do you want to write, 'Thanks a million, Mitch' on a sticky note? I'll make sure he gets it."

"Very funny, Naomi," I said with a sheepish smile. "I'll send him a telegram."

"Send it from an island," she called after me as I returned to my office. "You need a vacation." ▪

CHAPTER TWO

Bellwether by Way of *Blowback*

(2002-03)

I HAD JOINED CARLYLE NASH five years earlier, at the age of 28. I came in through the back door. My only previous magazine experience had been two years at a gun magazine in Deerfield Beach, Florida. As a proofreader and sometime writer at the esteemed *Blowback*, my job had been to take products that can obliterate organs and make them sound as innocuous as squash rackets.

The next entry on my résumé was local press relations and audition-running for a suburban murder-mystery dinner theater. So when Diane and I returned to New York, where we'd both grown up, so she could attend grad school, my prospects for landing any type of creative work beyond "boundary-pushing sandwich maker" didn't seem promising.

But timing really is everything. Just two days after my older brother Bobby told me at Easter dinner to "get serious, stop just sending out résumés, pound the pavement," I sat as the only warm, wet body in the waiting room of a Midtown temp agency; sustained rains had eliminated the day's rival job-seekers.

I dried off with Dunkin' Donuts napkins as the weary fifty-ish agency rep reviewed my résumé. She set it aside, licked a middle finger and began leafing through a short stack of assignment sheets.

"Let's see," she said, "I do have something pretty easy at... Here it is...*Bellwether*."

"Great. I worked in a hotel once."

She sighed and looked up.

"The magazine. *Bellwether*."

"Oh, the magazine. Of course, yes. Absolutely. *Bellwether*. What's the job?"

"Office stuff. Nothing too challenging."

"Great. I do have writing experience."

She glanced at her watch.

"That's wonderful. But don't get your hopes up. Just go. And fix your tie."

"Alright," I said as I stood up.

"Try not to drop your Rs."

Less than an hour later, I was on my way to meet the editorial business manager of the century-old literary weekly, the crown jewel of Carlyle Nash. While I had, in fact, heard of the magazine, I knew nothing about the parent company. The assignment was in the Editorial Business Department. The qualifications: punctuality and suit ownership.

For roughly 15 hours a week, I sat at a small wooden desk—no phone, no computer—rubber-stamping car-service receipts and travel-and-expense submissions for the magazine's staff of editors, writers, and cartoonists. Sure, I was overqualified, but it was a way into a company that was flush. With each expense report, I learned not only that there were people in the world who ate five meals a day, but that they could do so entirely at the expense of a money-burning corporate parent. Carlyle Nash, I thought, was a company I could work for.

I wanted to be a writer, but I figured out quickly that *Bellwether* wasn't handing out editorial jobs to pushing-thirty temps with high school newspaper clips and a *Blowback* feature on Year 2000's best assault rifles. Nor would they be interested in the three dog-eared, half-completed short stories I carried around in my backpack. That said, I could write, I was smart, and I'd been working harder than the kid next to me since the age of 11. No Ivy-League-bred Carlyle Nasher could match my résumé: paperboy, house painter, dishwasher, deli clerk, bar back, carpenter's helper, and the eighth of nine kids—a job in itself.

So I worked hard and fast, and I made friends on the business side. Word around the office was that the Marketing Department was expanding and a full-time coordinator position was opening up. Carol, the supervisor of Editorial Business, was generous enough to recommend me, and an interview was scheduled for the following week. She told me I had the inside track, because internal recommendations carried the most weight. She was also pretty tight with the human resources director. It would be tough to screw up.

I clinched the job when I told Pam, the HR rep, how the eccentric old Southerner who owned *Blowback* used to fire his Glock through the ceiling when he was in a bad mood.

"Then I suppose you can handle the pressure of *Bellwether*," she said with a smile.

I couldn't wait to tell Diane. Newlyweds, we were living in a Hicksville, Long Island apartment until we found decent jobs—the upstairs of a house owned by Keith and Renee Sadler. Renee worked a nondescript office job for a trucking company that allowed her to wear a velour tracksuit each day, while Keith was an air-conditioning repairman, biker and amateur heavy metal musician. When I arrived home just past dusk, his band, DarKStorm, was jamming in the open bay of the garage. They were playing the superior of their two original songs. Keith clearly hadn't washed up after work. His meaty hands were covered in grease. He hit a bad note on his bass guitar but glared at his drummer and yelled, "What the fuck?" over the stick-thin lead singer's vocals. I skipped the small talk, as he had recently raised our rent after I had shared my opinion that fans probably wouldn't understand that the capitalized, italicized KS in the band's name represented his initials. I instead smiled and flashed the sign of the horns as I passed by on my way to the exterior staircase at the back of the house. When I reached our second-story landing, the stray cat that had taken a liking to our weather-beaten patio furniture mustered a bored glance.

"Hey slob," I said, "if you don't start showing some gratitude, I'm gonna stop the Steak-umms."

Diane was sitting in the kitchen when I came in. The apartment was ordered and spotless as usual. Fresh flowers were in the center of the table. She was beaming.

"I got the paid internship!" she shouted as she sprang up and nearly tackled me with a hug.

"Yes! Thank God. I am so proud of you, honey."

I hugged her as she jumped up and down in my arms. Diane had been one of a fiercely competitive group of graduate students going for just two paid social-work internships at St. Joseph's Hospital. Landing it would allow her to leave her full-time survival job—our full-time survival job—as a receptionist at a doctor's office and focus on the work she loved while still being able to pay the bills and start saving for a house. After I shared my own good news of an impending full-time position, we opened a bottle of wine. Twenty-four hours earlier we had been up late talking about how we could be happy together doing anything: Lola and Tony at the Copa—the delusions of people without a mortgage. But we did know instinctively that a bigger world awaited us, and that hustle and a hopeful attitude would eventually vault us into it.

I took a Tombstone pizza out of the oven using a frayed dish towel as an oven mitt. I set it down to cool and picked up my wine glass.

"Be careful," she said. "There's a little chip on the rim of that one."

I turned the glass to a safe spot and raised a toast.

"To dollar stores. May we never enter one again."

* * * *

JUST OVER A YEAR into my first full-time job at Carlyle Nash, the publisher of *Bellwether* was moved out. Larry Gates had been an odd fit for a legendary literary magazine anyway. Thickheaded and thin-skinned, he had excelled only in the area of making quick decisions. That they were all puzzling ones—e.g., telling advertisers to "think of *Bellwether* as *Playboy* in its heyday, but without the skin"—sealed his fate after just 15 revenue-bleeding months. In fairness, he was just the latest in a line of publishers who couldn't pull the chronic money-loser of a magazine out of its 30-year tailspin.

Ten floors down, another magazine was undergoing a financial renaissance. *Fine Estates*, a shelter book for the super affluent, had reversed a decade-long revenue decline to not just post a profit but lead the company in year-over-year performance. Its publisher: a dashing prodigy named Mitch Blake, who was fast building a reputation as the industry's top turnaround man. We would all soon find out if he could take *Bellwether* into the black too. Larry Gates, meanwhile, would be swapped in at *Fine Estates*. In his stumbling farewell address he tried to spin the decision as a win for everyone, but it was really Carlyle Nash's familiar way of telling a failed publisher to start looking for a new job at a different company. Of course, I didn't realize that at the time.

The background and implications of the swap were explained to me by John Steffans, our cynical, war-weary Associate Publisher of Marketing. John emerged ashen-faced from his office when the news hit and headed straight for my cubicle. He handed me a sticky note with the words *Let's go* written on it. I mouthed "Now?" He nodded, hiked his trousers up over his belly, and was off. I waited two minutes before following.

John had taken an instant liking to me when I came on board—and the feeling was mutual. Having grown up with older brothers, I was comfortable with guys who had a few years on me. But mostly my fast friendship with the bespectacled Ohio native was based on three things in no certain order: our similar sense of humor, the quality of my work, and my ability to do that work half drunk. *Let's go* meant that I was to meet him at the lobby bar of the Midtown Millennium Hotel two blocks over. It was 11:30 AM.

"You don't understand," John said, washing down pretzels with his first gin and tonic. "Gates is done. They're just parking him at *Fine Estates* where he can't fuck anything up until they find his replacement. Watch, it will be a first-time publisher from the sales ranks. That douchebag Brendan Rush will get it. The guy has set up shop in the asshole of every Moreland, even Kent the fourth. I heard he blew him."

"You're kidding me? Kent? The intern?"

"Intern. Please. That kid's a billionaire already. Christ, I may have to blow him."

"What do you mean?"

"I'm done, Paul. Mitch Blake will do what every new publisher does. He'll bring in his own people."

"Shit. Should I be looking for a new job too?"

"No, no. You're safe. You're nobody. I mean, you'll be somebody someday, but not yet. I'm talking about directors and above. Blake knows my work, but it doesn't matter. He has his team of suck-ups at *Fine Estates* and each one of them will be eased in one by one. It's the way it goes. Worst-case scenario for you is if your new boss is an asshole. But you'll be fine."

John's cell phone rang. He recognized the number and muttered "This fucking motherfucker." As he took the call, I sat back in relief that he thought my job safe, but I was also a bit disappointed that my mentor was resigned to moving on. I took a sip of my Bass Ale and turned my attention to the muted television set above the bar. Six CNBC talking heads, with neck veins bulging above white collars, screamed in unison about their money. John, mostly listening to the caller, motioned for another round of drinks and a menu. I settled in for another long lunch courtesy of Calvin Moreland.

John ended the call a minute or two later with "OK, talk to you tomorrow." He tossed the phone on the bar. It bumped a few pretzels out of the bowl as it slid by.

"Shit," he said. "Simon wants me back."

Simon was Simon Bell, Carlyle's President of Corporate Sales, the division responsible for the marketing of the company as a whole. He had been trying to get John to come work for him in Corporate ever since the two had moved on from *Gloss*, Carlyle's flagship beauty magazine. Simon was a mercurial, high-maintenance executive whom John had vowed never to work for again, but he was a man who knew talent—and John had talent.

"I'm gonna have to work for him again."

"Is he really that bad?" I asked.

"He can be a lunatic. Demanding as hell. But he's charming too. Got me to where I am on salary. Loyal as a dog. Brilliant but insecure. I can't control his expectations and manipulate him like I could Gates."

"So you're going?"

"Yeah, it'll happen. He's got me where he wants me. If I don't go, Blake will dump me. I know it."

He paused and then brightened.

"Wait a minute, listen, despite what I said about Simon, you should come with me. Right after I get settled. You have to. Simon will love you. And I can get you some more money."

As flattered as I was by the thought, John had put me back on my heels. I knew intuitively that the right move for me was to sit tight where I was, gaining experience at a magazine potentially primed for a big turnaround under the hottest name in the building.

"Wow, thanks John," I said. "I think that could be great. Although I kind of want to see what happens here in the next month or two."

John looked me in the eye. I could sense his surprise that I wasn't more enthusiastic about following a boss whose primary demand of me was eating steak washed down with red wine. But he was underestimating my ambition.

"Of course," he said. "Not right away. Like I said, after I get settled."

"Great," I responded, picking up a menu. "Are we doing appetizers?" ▪

CHAPTER THREE

Tremors at *World*
(2007)

I GRABBED an available folding chair and found a patch of grass in the middle of Bryant Park. Surrounded by hordes of sun-seeking lunchgoers, I wasn't there to eat. I reached into my breast pocket and pulled out the *World* circulation memo Mitch had praised a few hours earlier. When it came to reveling in a well-executed assignment—especially one that pleased Mitch—few people could spend more time at it than I could. As far back as my first days at *Bellwether*, I had been indulging this ego-reinforcing habit. It drove Diane crazy. Reading and re-reading, over and over again, every sentence, each word. Patting myself on the back for a particularly useful competitive insight, or a data point others might have missed, or just a good turn of phrase.

The circulation memo had been strategic in nature. Its purpose was to prep our sales staff on how to discuss *World*'s expectations for both subscription and newsstand growth. This information was critical to advertisers because they wanted to know how soon *World* would be supported exclusively by readers who actually paid for the magazine. During the launch period of a new publication, copies are sent free to demographically screened prospective subscribers and placed in public places such as doctors' offices. If readers like the magazine, they'll hopefully convert to paying customers. The bottom line: if, after six to eight issues, a magazine is still relying on controlled distribution to meet the circulation level it has promised to advertisers, that magazine is in trouble.

My memo, distilling Mitch's comprehensive audience-building plan, aimed to dispel any doubts that *World* would enjoy real and rapid growth. I was confident in our projections that the magazine would be standing on its own by Issue Five. My mood had also been brightened by an unexpected late-morning meeting with clients from British Airways. Jim Keane had called me in when the four-member team started peppering him with circulation questions. I had taken them through a PowerPoint overview of our projections and the session had ended with smiles and handshakes. As I now soaked in the sun, the day felt like it was turning.

My Blackberry rang. John was calling. I was tempted to answer but I had to get back to work on my *Globalist* presentation. After one last satisfied read of my memo, I played back his voicemail: "Hey asshole, I'm at Donovan's. The bar in the back. Terry is working. Come. Now."

Donovan's was eight blocks and two avenues away. Over the years, John had befriended every bartender in Manhattan who gave away the house. Terry was one such barkeep, but the drawback was Donovan's location. Too far today. Plus, I wasn't in the mood to hear John's incessant bashing of Mitch and *World*'s first issue, which I thought alright but he deemed awful. The corporate division in general—still led by Simon with John heading up marketing—may have been saying the right things in support of *World*, but, in truth, Simon hated Mitch for breaking his longstanding single-issue ad-page record. He had it in for *World* as much as any of our outside competitors did.

I closed my eyes to enjoy a few minutes of early summer sun.

As I leaned back, I heard Paige's voice.

"Why are you avoiding me?" she asked, pulling up a chair. She was a bit hoarse from her screaming match with Thad.

"I'm not avoiding you, I'm just..."

"You know you're avoiding me, but I forgive you. I'm driving everyone crazy. Phil and the kids want me to quit."

"You can't quit, Paige. Just hang in there for the rest of the year, then you can look to move internally."

"I know, I know, but I think Mitch hates me. I mean, I guess I don't know what he thinks. What do you think he thinks?"

"If I had a dollar for every person who doesn't know exactly where they stand with Mitch, I'd be a billionaire."

Paige was new to Carlyle Nash. She was one of several former *Globalist* staffers Mitch had poached for their pre-launch competitive intelligence. Now that we had launched *World*, many of them had begun to grow concerned that their usefulness had an expiration date. Aware that I had worked for Mitch at *Bellwether*, Paige and others often sought my opinion on where they stood with him. As if I knew. But I always tried to affect a calm, been-there-done-that air despite the fact that I never truly felt secure in Mitch's universe, either.

"It's just so frustrating," Paige went on, as she tied her straight black hair in a ponytail. "I can't take it anymore. And, my God, even if I could, the first issue was a mess."

"What are you talking about? I thought it was pretty good overall."

"Well, whatever you thought, some really bad press just hit. Didn't you see *Media Times*?"

"No."

"They called it 'an inaccessible, overstuffed luxury goods catalogue masquerading as a magazine.'"

"Shit," I said, "I missed that. Mitch must be pissed."

"I told you there were too many ads. I heard the Chicago focus groups hated it. Two people said it reminded them of *Town and Country*. One guy asked the moderator why anyone would think the world needed a news magazine exclusively for rich assholes. Watch the videos. You'll cry."

"I didn't know they were in yet. Fuck. I will."

"Oh, and Maserati is pissed that their ad ran next to the article on Haitian food riots."

As Paige sunk her teeth into an apple, I felt a creeping paranoia. Mitch had to have known all this when we'd spoken that morning. Why had he seemed so calm? Why hadn't he told me? Had he been waiting for me to say something? Testing to see if I was on top of things? How come Paige knew all this and I didn't? Wasn't I part of his inner circle anymore? And the beach ball. Was he anticipating advertiser flight because of bad press? Was that the reason for offering another incentive? I stood up and grabbed my suit jacket off the chair.

"We should get back, Paige."

"Go ahead without me," she said as she gave up on the apple and placed it on the grass. "I'm going to sit here and think about what I want to do with my miserable life."

"Don't worry. Everything will be fine."

* * * *

WHEN I GOT BACK to the office, there were three messages waiting. One from John, who had moved on to the bar at the Millennium. One from Thad, which I deleted at "Paul, I need an analysis of—." And one from Diane: "Just wanted to let you know that I landed safely. I'm sure you've been beside yourself with worry. Don't forget that you have to take Aidan to the pediatrician on Tuesday. Call me if you have to. It's beautiful here. Maybe someone will have sex with me."

My email pinged. Mitch: *Please stop by*. I grabbed a pad and headed down to his office. Naomi was standing at her desk as I approached, talking to someone on the phone. She raised her index finger, signaling me to wait.

"Mitch said it's because of a product recall. Something in the plastic. Or the dyes. Or the card. I don't know. Anyway, if they haven't gone out to the outside offices, just bring them up from the mailroom...They haven't? OK, good, just send them up. Thanks."

"What's that all about?" I asked.

"Where have you been? Mitch needs you. Total shit storm right now."

My heart began to race. My left eyelid twitched.

"Sorry. Well I'm here now. Can I go in?"

"Wait a minute. He's on the phone with Jimmy. Can you believe Josh Sherman quit? One issue and done."

"You're kidding me."

"I heard he called Jimmy a douchebag on the way out. My fantasy."

Jimmy Stillman was *World's* editor-in-chief. A high-profile prodigy recruited from *New York Now*, he was hired largely to put a youthful face on a magazine category traditionally run by old white guys. All of our established competitors, including *The Globalist* and *Currents*, were edited by ink-stained industry vets. Jimmy had never been an editor-in-chief, but he wrote a buzzy column at *NYN* and that was enough for Calvin Moreland, who typically hired the hot name. Word had been getting around that the editorial side was twice as pressure-packed as the business side, and that Jimmy wasn't the easiest person to work for. The departure of Josh Sherman, his deputy editor, was proof of that. I could hear Mitch wrapping up the call in a reassuring tone.

"Don't worry, Jimmy. The more ambitious a launch, the more the knives come out. We'll be fine. I'm not worried in the slightest...OK, talk to you later."

I inched toward the threshold. Mitch looked up, but as usual didn't make entirely direct eye contact. In the rare moments when he wasn't multitasking, his conversational gaze seemed to subtly flit from my forehead to my upper lip. It could be unsettling—I often wondered if that was intentional—but I'd mostly grown used to it.

"Paul, come in."

He seemed outwardly calm, which I did my best to mirror.

"Hi, Mitch. What can I do for you?"

"Providence Insurance. We had them locked up for twelve pages from September through December but they're thinking of backing out. I need you to do a turnaround paper. Hit on the importance of innovation and buzz, reassure them on the circulation strategy, hammer *Currents*... You know, talk them off the ledge. Drop anything else you're working on. Can you get it to me by the time I land in San Francisco?"

"No problem, Mitch. I'll get started."

"OK. And if you see Paige, tell her I'm looking for her."

"Will do, Mitch."

As I backpedaled, Naomi squeezed past.

"Mitch," she said, "I've got Lou Lamont on the line."

Mitch grabbed the receiver with a somewhat nervous quickness I'd never seen from him before.

"Lou, my man..."

He motioned for us to shut the door on our way out. As Naomi sat down, I leaned on her desk.

"By the way," I asked, "what were you talking about on the phone before... Some kind of product recall on the beach balls?"

"Oh, yeah. You have to return yours too. But I think he's going to have Paige collect them. Just hang on to it for now, I guess."

When I got back to my office, I picked up my beach ball, squeezed and pondered it. *Product recall? Something in the plastic?* The whole thing struck me as odd. My eyes wandered to the companion incentive card I'd pinned up earlier. I pulled it down and placed it in my breast pocket. I dropped the beach ball into my briefcase. ▪

CHAPTER FOUR

The *Bellwether* Introduction

(2003)

YOU ALWAYS HOPE for an express elevator ride when returning from lunch drunk. You don't always get one.

John and I had timed our return from the Millennium bar so we would be back at *Bellwether* by 2:30. The usual strategy. The hour was not so late that it was overly noticeable but late enough that we could usually exhale gin and beer in our very own elevator car. And it allowed us one more drink, of course, before heading back. As we waited in the lobby for a car to arrive, John silently handed me a stick of gum. The elevator directly behind me dinged.

"Go," he said.

We moved into the empty car and I quickly pressed the 17 button while John hit "Door Close" on the opposite panel. I pressed the same button again on my side as a rushed clickety-clack of high heels approached. The doors closed just in time. Chivalry, I noted with guilt, was for the sober.

As we began our ascent, I slipped into mildly slurred work-speak.

"I'll finish up that Toyota presentation by tomorrow. Do you need to see it?"

"Fuck no. I don't give a shit."

The car slowed to a stop on the seventh floor. I reflexively looked up at the horizontal line of numbers and corresponding magazine names above: "7–FINE ESTATES."

The doors opened and on stepped the soon-to-be-publisher of *Bellwether*, Mitch Blake. He locked in on John, who was looking down at his phone to avoid whoever had boarded.

"John Steffans," he said as he extended his hand, "I'm glad to finally run into you."

A startled John looked up.

"Mitch...Mitch. Oh, hey, hi Mitch. Welcome. To *Bellwether*, I mean. Not the elevator."

John glanced over at me, as if to include me in the exchange, but I didn't respond. I stared straight ahead and adopted the body language of a mere fellow traveler who just happened to be on the same elevator as the gin-soaked executive. My posture screamed *I'm not with him. I haven't been out to lunch. I was just down at the company library doing important research...on my way back from a quality check in production... A young up-and-comer making things happen.* I pressed a random button: 15–TRUE GENT.

Mitch paid me no mind.

"Very funny," he said to John. "Good to be here—at *Bellwether* and on your elevator. Hey, it'll be great to work with you. I'm heading up to talk transition with Gates right now. Why don't you get on my calendar for tomorrow?"

"Sure. Sounds good, Mitch. I will."

John glanced up at the elevator's progress, willing it to move faster, just as we stopped on 15. I stepped to the front and prepared to get off, almost pressing my nose against the doors. I knew I had taken my ridiculously paranoid play-acting too far by pressing 15, but I had no choice other than to complete the charade by getting off. I hoped John would do the math and realize that I didn't want my first introduction to my new publisher to be a drunken one. The doors opened.

"Where are you going, Paul?" said John.

His tone dripped with mischief.

"Oh, I was just stopping by *True Gent* to borrow their, uh, IntelliQuest survey code book."

"We have an IntelliQuest code book."

I scratched my forehead as I stood on the elevator threshold. John, seeming miraculously sober and focused, turned to Mitch.

"Mitch, let me introduce you to Paul Cavanaugh. He works for me."

Mitch extended his hand. I quickly wiped mine on my trouser leg and reached in.

"Very nice to meet you, Mitch. I look forward to you coming on bloard...board."

"Good to meet you too. Where have you guys been, by the way?"

John jumped in.

"Lunch with a vendor. Those party boys over at Monroe Research. Two drinks and they start cutting their rates. Right, Paul?"

"You said it, John. Anyway, I'll see you in five. Nice to meet you again, Mitch."

Mitch leaned against the back wall of the elevator and nodded once.

"See you Monday," he said.

I stepped back and the doors began to close. John stuck his foot between them and they slid open.

"Hey, Paul. One more thing. Get me that Toyota presentation by close of business. It's three days late."

I could feel my face flush as the doors closed.

"Unbelievable," I moaned as I circled to the stairwell and began climbing the two flights to our floor. My footfalls echoed loudly as I fumbled for my key card. When I emerged into the hallway, the stairway entry door slammed shut behind me. A few cubicled colleagues glanced at their watches as I passed by. I headed straight for John's office and found him with his feet up already, laughing hard.

"Close the door."

"You son of a bitch," I said as I slid it shut.

"I didn't know you were such a pussy, Paul."

"Come on, you would have done the same thing if you were me. I couldn't let that be his first impression. But now it's too late."

"For God's sake," said John as he reached into the freezer section of his mini-fridge, "He won't even remember your name when he starts. And you're coming with me to Corporate anyway. After I 'get on Mitch's calendar' of course. What fucking bullshit that was. It would have been refreshing if he had just canned me on the elevator."

He began pouring two glasses of chilled vodka.

"Jesus," I said, "I don't need more booze. Are you trying to poison me or something?"

"Just fucking drink it. We're on vacation until that jerk-off starts. Enjoy it."

I took a sip and instantly felt like throwing up. It wasn't vodka.

"Fuck. What the hell is this?"

"It's moonshine. My son makes it in his dorm room."

I knew John liked to drink, but this was getting ridiculous.

"I have to get out of here, John. I really do have work to do."

"You're such a goody-goody, Paul."

"Goody-goody? I've had three beers, a glass of wine, an Irish coffee, and now some rubbing alcohol. I'm done, man."

"Breakfast in Ohio… Fine, go. Leave the door shut. Wake me at five and we'll go to Donovan's."

They say you should never make major decisions drunk, but

I knew for sure in that moment that I wouldn't be following John to Corporate. Diane and I needed a house. It was time to get serious. To "buckle down," as my Dad might have put it. I would do my buckling down at *Bellwether*. ▪

CHAPTER FIVE

Disconnected at *World*

(2007)

WITH MITCH IN San Francisco terrifying *World's* West Coast reps with his mere presence, I decided to "work from home" on Monday. Thad was on the road too, so I figured I could pull it off without either of them knowing. It gave me the option of spending a third straight day alone with Aidan, but I had no intention of doing that. I needed a break, even if just to take an aimless drive or maybe to hit a few golf balls at the range. I called my mother and told her I would drop Aidan off at her house because mine was a mess with Diane away. I threw on a suit so she would think I was headed into the office. It was the same one I had worn Friday—wrinkled a bit from having spent the weekend balled up on my basement pool table, but otherwise passable. As I climbed the basement stairs, I ran my hands down the front of the jacket to smooth the wrinkles and felt something in my breast pocket. I pulled it out. It was the incentive card. The events of Friday rushed in. The day had been a difficult one for *World*, but I had found a personal port in the storm. I had written my turnaround paper for Providence Insurance in a flash and had known immediately that it was one of the best I'd ever done. As usual, I hadn't even been thinking about whether it would change the client's mind as much as just hoping it would please Mitch. When he emailed me at midnight on Friday, *Good. Thx*, I knew I had nailed the assignment. Still, I had woken up this morning wondering why he hadn't spelled out *thanks*. And why not *Great*? Or *Nice job, Paul*? Did *Good* just mean good enough?

Stop, stop, stop it, I told myself as I stuck the incentive card to the refrigerator door with a pineapple-shaped magnet—right next to a doctor's appointment reminder card for Aidan's checkup. His appointment was tomorrow. I had completely forgotten about it.

"Fuck."

I couldn't possibly take off two days in a row, especially with Mitch returning to the office the next day. I would have to cancel the appointment. Diane would be furious, but I felt I had no choice.

Aidan began stirring in his crib so I grabbed a bottle of breast milk from the refrigerator and placed it in a marinara-stained Tupperware bowl filled with hot water. Empty beer bottles clanked and fell in the sink as I cleared space. A few cheddar Goldfish floated in a rocks glass I didn't remember using.

Aidan was cooing happily when I entered his room. His diaper was around his right ankle, his legs adorned with feces.

"Damn, boy," I said as I opened the blinds and cracked a window.

I gathered him up, crib bedding and all, and headed for the tub. He smiled up at me with ignorant adoration and I kissed him on the head.

"I still love you, chunky man."

After I had hosed him down in the tub like an inmate, toweled him dry and put him in a clean diaper and onesie, I strapped him in the bouncy chair he was fast outgrowing and loaded up a Baby Einstein DVD. He strained against the chair's tightly buckled harness and screamed "Mo, Emmo!"

"Alright, alright," I said as I freed him. He stumbled over to a plush Elmo-themed kiddie chair and fell in.

He wasn't demanding his bottle just yet so I banked the time and picked up my Blackberry. The first unread email was from Thad, reminding me that I was on the sales meeting agenda for Wednesday. I delightedly responded that Mitch had told me to drop everything for the turnaround paper, so I would need at least another week. I closed with *I hope you die in a plane crash*, savored the line for a moment, then deleted it and hit *send*.

"I still hope you die in a plane crash," I muttered.

I scrolled through a few unimportant emails from colleagues: *Can I get five minutes with you on a BMW pitch?* *Is there a one-sheet on public place circulation?* *I want to kill myself*—from Paige.

Delete, delete, and *Don't do it without me.* Then, an email from Mitch. The subject line read *Tomorrow.* I sighed and set the Blackberry down. Aidan began crying for his bottle so I got up and gave it to him. I returned to the kitchen table, picked up the Blackberry and dropped it to the floor. It wasn't the first time I had dropped it, but this time when I picked it up, a blank charcoal-gray screen stared back. I furiously pressed a few buttons, tried every control-command-shift-alt reset in the book, and nearly gave it mouth-to-mouth...but nothing.

"Oh, Jesus Christ!" I screamed.

The phone rang. I scurried across the kitchen to check the Caller ID. The message light was blinking too, reminding me that I hadn't called my sister Ellen back on Sunday after screening her all weekend. The ID read "CSH Pediatrics," so I picked up.

"Hello."

"Hello, Mr. Cavanaugh?"

"Yes."

"This is Cold Spring Pediatrics calling to confirm Aidan's appointment for tomorrow."

"I have to cancel that."

"Oh, OK. When is a good day?"

"Whenever."

"Well, we actually just had a cancellation for eleven a.m. today. Would that work?"

I had a vision of Diane at a swim-up bar in Puerto Rico. If I told her that the pediatrician had canceled the appointment himself, she would surely call the office to verify. But then I imagined her laughing with her friends and ordering another daiquiri. A shirtless Javier Bardem was massaging her neck. Fuck it.

"No. Today's no good. I'll call you back to reschedule."

I hung up and looked over at Aidan. A pang of guilt hit me as I watched him suck on his bottle, swaying in front of the television. But he did look as strong as an ox. Was it that big a deal to move a routine checkup back a week or two? Diane would have to understand about the critical turn of events at *World*.

After Aidan finished his bottle, I threw together a bag of baby essentials and dropped him off at my mother's house. That I was heading to Manhattan solely to read an email from Mitch did register to me as ridiculous...but only for a moment.

* * * *

I WAS SWEATING WHEN I ARRIVED at *World* just before noon. I slung my suit jacket over my shoulder as I made a sharp right through the glass doors and past the freighter-sized *World* logo mounted at the entry. The letters looked like they were formed from African elephant tusks. Three separate font consultants had worked on the design of the W alone.

Lily Kober, the senior of two marketing managers who reported to me, sat up in surprise as I passed her cubicle outside my office.

"I thought you were working from home," she said as she followed me in, sat down, and pushed her glasses atop her head.

"I *was* working from home. But I have to deal with a Mitch thing. And my Blackberry is down."

"You know, Matt and I can handle things, Paul. You're allowed to take a day off."

"I know, I know. But I just had to get here. Hard to explain."

"I can explain it. You're insane. How's Aidan?"

"He thinks I'm insane too."

I logged into my email to read the *Tomorrow* message from Mitch. Lily shifted in her seat.

"Can we talk about my review? I've been waiting three weeks."

"Shit. I'm sorry, Lily. I totally forgot. But I have good news."

I rifled through a stack of in-box items and pulled out a yellow interoffice envelope from Human Resources. I pulled out a memo confirming an eight-percent raise. She deserved it for keeping the sales hounds at bay while I catered to Mitch. As I handed her the memo, I knew she would think I had fought for the number on her behalf, but in fact HR was in rubber-stamp mode. I asked for eight percent, they asked if she was good, I said yes, and they approved it. I could have gotten 10.

"Oh my God," Lily said, "This is great. Thanks so much Paul. But one question. How long has this been sitting under a stack of junk mail?"

"I don't know. A week maybe. Listen, I'm an asshole. I've just been crazed. Sorry."

"I forgive you. But this is why you need a day off!"

"Fine, fine. Now get out. Go buy me a bottle of wine in appreciation."

"That's the last thing you need," she said as she turned on my electric desk fan and angled it at my head.

"Oh, that feels great. Thanks. Now go away."

I located Mitch's email and braced for impact. I was sure he would be asking for another turnaround paper. A wave of relief washed over me as I saw that it was addressed to *CNWORLD-ALL*. It read:

A couple of curveballs came our way on Friday, but it's nothing we can't handle. I know how hard each of you has been working, so please join me in the large conference room for breakfast tomorrow. Come hungry. I guarantee you'll leave happy. —Mitch

I pushed my chair back and smiled weakly, noting how right Lily was. I really did need a day off. The phone rang and I saw that it was John—calling from Corporate. I had declined his last five lunch requests because I wanted to walk the line during work hours. Running down to Mitch's office with a headful of data was stressful enough for me sober. But Mitch wouldn't be landing until evening. I turned the fan down a setting and picked up.

"I can do it. Where to?"

"Holy shit," said John. "I guess that means you already gave Mitch his hand job today."

"He's in San Francisco. Thank God. But he's back tonight. You would think he'd spend an extra day. Go to fucking Fisherman's Wharf or something. Like a normal person."

"Simon's out too. Let's go to that shitty little Mexican place on Forty-fourth. Finance is bitching about my expenses."

"Fine. I could go for a Margarita."

"Great. Twelve-fifteen. Don't be late."

Paige had been standing in the doorway. She was holding a clipboard.

"This is why I went to Princeton," she sighed. "To round up beach balls. Do you have yours?"

"You're kidding me, right? He really wants them back? Just tell me to throw it in the trash and I will."

"I know. It's so stupid. But he said he doesn't want anyone's kid licking it or something."

The phone rang. It was my brother Rich.

"It's around here somewhere, Paige. I'll give it to you after lunch. I have to take this call."

"OK. Don't forget."

As Paige turned, I pressed my secondary line and said, "This is Paul" to an imaginary caller. I let my brother go to voicemail. I was sure my mother was spreading the word among my siblings about how stressed I seemed of late. But as important as they were to me, I just didn't want to face eight variations of "What the hell is going on with you?"

It was 12:05. I put my head in my hands and stared for a few seconds at the framed photo I kept on my desk of Aidan on his first day in the world—swaddled in his standard-issue blue-and-white hospital blanket, eyes at half-mast.

I'm an asshole.

I called John and said "Let's go." ▪

CHAPTER SIX

Bellwether Signs
(2005)

A S THE LAWYERS passed papers back and forth across the table, I leaned to my left and whispered in Diane's ear.

"Those last two you signed were actually your commitment papers."

"If anyone belongs in an institution, it's you," she whispered back.

I squeezed her hand underneath the table before signing another check and handing it over to my lawyer. I had stopped asking what they were even for.

He slid it across to his counterpart and then turned to shake our hands.

"Paul, Diane, we are closed. You've got yourself a house."

We shook hands with everyone around the table and made small talk with the sellers. After they exited the conference room, Diane and I hugged.

"We did it!" she said.

"I can't believe it. Let's go pack up all our shit right now."

"OK, but let's sleep one last night in the apartment. It'll

be romantic."

"Yes, by all means. One more night of death metal and squalor."

As we embraced, Diane felt the vibration of my Blackberry. She deftly reached into my breast pocket and snatched it.

"Oh, come on, Diane," I said. "I told you I wouldn't read emails. Give it back."

"That's right. You're not going to read emails. I'll only give it back if you promise me."

"I promise, I swear."

She opened my coat and put the phone back in my breast pocket. I held her face and kissed her. Her auburn ringlets brushed the backs of my hands. She wrapped her arms around my waist.

"I love you," she said. "You big jerk."

"I love you too."

I pulled away, reached for the Blackberry, and ran to the opposite side of the table.

"I'll just look at the subject line, I swear!"

"You're ridiculous!" Diane shouted. "Fine. I'm going to the ladies' room. Read your stupid email and then figure out where you're taking me to dinner."

"I will. I love you."

The subject line of the email read *Huge Win*. It was from Grace Browning, *Bellwether*'s New England sales rep, and it was addressed to Mitch. I was cc'd along with three colleagues and my new marketing boss, Michael Pace. John had been right when he had predicted that he wouldn't be long at *Bellwether* after Mitch came in, but Simon had swept him up quickly. The email read:

Hi, Mitch. I just wanted to share the great news that we landed Volkswagen. 20-page schedule. Will call you with all the details. Thanks to the whole team and a big shout-out to Paul. The presentation and research were spot-on. Thanks, Grace.

I pumped my fist and reveled in the roll *Bellwether* was on.

This was the third big win of the week. The magazine's first profitable year in decades was in our sights. As I emailed a thank you for the shout-out to Grace, a reply-all email from Mitch arrived:

Great news, GB. Call u in 5. Michael: bring copy of presentation to management mtg. Good work, Pal.

"What the fuck?" I said as I fell into a chair. "That's it?"

I read the email again. *Good work, Pal?* Was he praising Michael—who hadn't even seen the presentation, much less worked on it—or had he misspelled my name? The capital P made me think he did mean me, but maybe not. Either way, it was infuriating. Why not ask *me* to drop off a copy of the presentation? He knew full well that Michael was just an administrator, the guy who made the trains run on time in marketing.

I let out an audible "Arrggghh" as my lawyer came back in to retrieve a file.

"Hey, you have a house now. You'll be making that sound every day."

"Yeah," I said. "Just dealing with some BS at work."

"Go celebrate, man."

He kissed Diane goodbye as they passed each other in the doorway. Her smile disappeared the second she saw me slumped and serious. I put the Blackberry away but it vibrated immediately. I took it out again and saw a response from Michael.

"For God's sake," said Diane. "I knew this would happen."

"No, no, no. It's all good. We won Volkswagen and I—"

"I don't care, Paul."

"Please, Diane. Just read one thing for me and then we're done. I just want your opinion. Then you can hold the Blackberry for the rest of the day."

"OK. Deal," she said sitting down. "But this is ridiculous."

"Thank you. Thank you. Here. Scroll down."

Diane read both emails.

"OK, great. And Mitch told you 'Good job.' Can we go now?"

"But it says 'Pal.' Did he misspell 'Paul' or is he calling Michael his 'Pal'?"

"Oh my God, you've lost your mind. Paul…please…your presentation helped land a huge account. Mitch knows. We've been through this before. He's always focused on the next thing. Michael has gotten you two nice raises. Stop it."

"You're right. I know. It's just annoying because I did that presentation alone from start to finish on a day's notice. That's what I want Mitch to know. But, no, I have to deal with this ridiculous hierarchy. Who knows how Michael frames things in the management meeting? He'll probably say he wrote the presentation and I just put it into PowerPoint. Let me just read his response."

I grabbed the Blackberry and read aloud.

"Will do, Mitch. Great team effort everyone. —Mike"

Diane sighed as she slowly took the Blackberry back and put it in her purse.

"This is the way it works, Paul. Someday you'll be Michael, someone else will be you, and you'll have precious Mitch all to yourself. But be careful what you wish for."

"I know. You're right."

"I'm always right," she said as she took my hand and pulled me up. "Did you think of a place for dinner?"

"Wherever you want."

"Why do I always have to pick the restaurant?"

* * * *

MICHAEL LEFT THE OFFICE for a long weekend just before noon on Thursday. John, with psychic/alcoholic timing for such things, called me for lunch. We couldn't decide where to go, so we said we'd meet in the lobby. I arrived first and leaned against a column, watching the comings and goings of one impeccably dressed Carlyle Nasher after another. John strode through a turnstile and gave a casual salute from a distance. A few paces behind him emerged a striking couple: Mitch and his wife, Danica. Mitch was wearing a seersucker suit with a peach tie. Danica, in a knee-length yellow dress and a sun hat, was carrying a Shih Tzu with a matching yellow bow.

"Where to?" asked John.

I ignored the question because Mitch had seen me and was approaching. John turned to see who I was looking at.

Mitch glanced at John and said, "Hey," as if barely remembering that he had fired him two years earlier. I could only hope my own drunken elevator introduction to Mitch was a distant memory too.

"Um...Paul," he said—almost as a question, as if he wasn't entirely sure I was indeed *the* Paul from the countless group emails he read each day. "Stop by my office at three. Michael's out and I need you to step in on a project."

"Absolutely, Mitch. I'll see you then."

He glanced at John and then back in my direction.

"Enjoy your lunch, guys."

The way he said it made me think that he did, in fact, remember our original introduction. It shouldn't have mattered so much, but I was still mortified that he might consider me some sort of party boy. Mitch was not a drinker.

He turned back to Danica and extended his arm. She slipped hers inside it and they floated away.

"Did you know that Simon dated her?" said John. "He told me she's frigid."

"I can't go to lunch," I said, breathless.

"Oh come on. What...you have to go *prepare*? You don't even know what he wants to talk about."

"I know. But I can't drink either."

"Just have one. Or...Jesus...none. You have to eat."

"I'm sorry, John," I said as I backpedaled to the elevators. "Maybe we can meet later?"

"I don't know. I have to—"

"Great," I shouted back. "I'll call you."

* * * *

I HAD MOSTLY LOST MY APPETITE after Mitch's invite, so I ate a banana and a handful of pretzels as I reviewed every recent project the department had worked on. I wanted to make sure I knew the answer to any question Mitch might ask—everything from our readers' median investable assets to the ad-page totals across the entire industry. During the final 10 minutes, I closed the door to my small interior office and practiced deep breathing. I was as ready as I could be. At 2:57, I slipped on my suit jacket and headed down the hall.

Mitch was wrapping up a meeting with Erik Belkin, one of our sales reps. He motioned me to come in, and I sat down in the chair next to Erik's. On the wall behind Mitch was a framed *Media Times* cover story: "Publisher of the Year—*True Gent*'s Mitch Blake." A few feet over was another: "Hot Sheet 2000 Magazine of the Year: *Fine Estates*." The photo showed Mitch and the magazine's editor-in-chief smoking cigars. Mitch's hair was gelled back like Gordon Gekko's, and he was clenching his cigar in a toothy, the-world-is-mine grin.

"Oh, just one more thing," said Erik. "Did you see this feature in the *Herald* on smart being the new hot?"

He passed a copy to Mitch.

"They even quote a study saying that eighty-five percent of brands want to advertise in more intellectual environments next year. We can really use that!"

He turned to me and I nodded.

Mitch smiled.

"Good catch, Erik. Send that around to the team."

"Will do, Mitch," said Erik as he bounded out happily.

Mitch tossed the article in the trash.

"Did you work on that study with Michael?"

"Excuse me?" I asked.

I could feel my face redden. I had prepared for virtually every possible question, but I had no idea what he meant.

"The study in the article. I had Michael conduct that. I thought he might have looped his team in."

"Oh...no he didn't tell us. I guess because we're always so busy with the day-to-day stuff."

"It's OK. Anyway, we hired a friendly polling firm to produce it. Our name is nowhere near it, of course. This way our reps can back up our 'Brains Are Back' positioning with some independent-sounding data."

"Ohhhh, I see."

I felt like an idiot. Sweat beaded above my upper lip.

"That's the game," he went on as he leafed through various papers, barely looking up. "Or at least it's the game we need to play. Anyway, listen. I want you to take the study and whatever other supporting press and data points you can find and knock out a one-sheet 'Brains Are Back' positioning piece. There's some ammo in the general presentation you can repurpose too, but make sure it's concise—something the reps can leave behind after a sales call. Can you send it to me first thing tomorrow?"

"Of course, Mitch."

He took a phone call.

"Lou Lamont, my man. Did you get that *Herald* article I sent over? Interesting study they quote. The *Tribune* should be on that. You're getting beaten to the punch."

Mitch gave me a thumbs-up without lifting his head. I gave him a thumbs-up back and then began tapping my fingers lightly on my notebook. As he listened to Lou, he turned and took a bottle of water from his fridge. He spun his chair back around and saw me still seated.

"You can go now," he whispered. •

CHAPTER SEVEN

A Theft at *World*
(2007)

"**W**E NEED SOME WOMEN HERE,**"** said John, as a second pitcher of margaritas arrived.

"Yeah, but it's only two-thirty," I said.

"You won't be able to get anyone to come over until four-thirty at the earliest. And you might be in jail by then."

"I can get Amanda and Jennie to come."

As he scrolled through his cell phone contacts, I poured a fresh glass and grabbed a few more tortilla chips.

"Why do I keep eating these? And why do they keep bringing them? We already ate."

"They keep bringing them because you keep eating them, moron."

"I'm being courteous. I keep eating them because they keep bringing them."

John picked up the bowl and gave it to a passing waiter.

"You can stop bringing these. Thanks."

He punched out a quick email and hit *send*.

"Can I borrow that for a second?" I asked. "Mine is dead."

"Good for you," he said as he slid the phone across.

I called Lily and asked her to get a tech guy to stop by my office to fix mine. She reminded me that I had already asked her to do that on my way out to lunch. The phone had been re-suscitated and was sitting quietly on my desk, she added. Mitch was mercifully offline, likely in the air en route from San Francisco. As I ended the call, an email arrived. I slid the phone back to John.

"It's from Amanda," he announced. "Let's see… 'Hi, John. We can't be there until five-thirty. We work for a living…' Fuck."

"I think I can meet at five."

"You can? Don't you have to get home to your kid?"

"I'm calling my mother. I could use a night out."

"Great," said John, as he leaned back and adjusted his belt. "Jennie is adorable. You'll like her."

"Does she work in Corporate?"

"Simon's assistant. Covers my ass when he's trying to find me. She's great."

I took a sip of my drink and stood up.

"You're not going back, right?" I asked. "I'm just running to my office to get my phone and my bag."

"Nope. This shit hole is my office today."

John eyed my jacket.

"You might want to invest in an iron, Paul."

"I only put this on today because I—oh, fuck it. Long story. I'll be right back."

I speedwalked, head down, through the parking garage linking 44th and 43rd Streets. Crossing 43rd, I zigzagged between the usual blockade of black town cars picking up and dropping off editors and executives. As I entered a revolving door, Lily was exiting through the other side on her way to lunch. She rapped on the glass as we slowly spun.

"Thad got back early," she said through the glass panel. "He's looking for you."

"I'm gonna work from home after all. Not feeling great."

She rolled her eyes but smiled.

"OK, Paul. Something tells me I'll be earning that raise."

"Exactly," I said as I emerged into the lobby, stumbling slightly.

Just two tasks remained before I could return to wasting away in Margaritaville: call my mother and avoid Thad. The first I could do later, of course, but the second could be a challenge. Whenever Mitch was on the road, Thad either went clothes shopping or patrolled the halls of *World* like a generalissimo.

I managed to make it to my office unseen. I grabbed my revived Blackberry and slipped it in my pocket, then circled behind the desk to pick up my bag from the floor. A purple sticky note was on my computer monitor, dead center. In thick black Sharpie ink it screamed: *NEED YOU IN FISH BOWL FOR AUDI CONFERENCE CALL NOW!!!! —THAD.*

"Shit. Fuck," I said as I crumpled the note.

I shut the door to my office to think of an escape plan, but quickly concluded that I had no choice but to join the meeting late. If I didn't, Thad would no doubt figure out that I had come back for my things, and then he would tell Mitch that I had been MIA for the day.

I had known about the Audi meeting but had told Thad's new assistant—a dim-looking kid named Jake—to leave me off the invite list because I had a conflict. I also knew that Audi had some concerns about the *World* circulation strategy, and I didn't feel up to spinning numbers I was beginning to question myself. I set my bag on my chair and headed for the fish bowl, a small glass-enclosed conference room on the opposite side of the floor. When I was about 10 paces away I saw only Thad, feet up on the table, talking hands free. I was surprised he was the only representative from our side. I slipped in, mouthed "Sorry I'm late," and sat down. He was wrapping up a thought.

"...Well, I guess that's how we would need to approach it. I'll get the process moving."

A somewhat muffled but familiar voice responded.

"Yes, we have to deal with it."

It was Mitch. I nearly gagged. My mellow Margarita buzz vanished.

"Here's Paul," said Thad. "So glad you could join us."

"Paul," said Mitch. "Why weren't you in the Audi meeting? Thad said he could have used you."

"Sorry, Mitch," I stammered, "but I wasn't on the invite. I just found out about it."

This was a half-truth, of course. That it was coming out of my mouth, and to Mitch of all people, shook me a bit. White lies—heck, even bald-faced lies—were routine throughout Carlyle Nash, but I had always clung to a personal code of accountability and honesty. Certainly with Mitch. That code, however, was becoming increasingly difficult for me to honor.

"Alright," said Mitch. "Thad, make sure you've got the right people at the table for client meetings. This shouldn't have happened."

Thad flushed and glared at me.

"I'm sorry, Mitch. I thought he was invited. I'll check with my assistant. But I did try to track Paul down. He was out. Isn't that right, Paul?"

"Yes. I was at physical therapy. I tore my left meniscus."

This was a fractional truth. I *had* torn my meniscus...in a pick-up football game on Thanksgiving of 1995. The extent of my physical therapy at the time had been the application of an iced can of Budweiser held in place by an Ace bandage.

"Oh," said Thad. "Lily told me you were at lunch."

"Right, yeah, after physical therapy. A quick bite."

Mitch cut in.

"Alright. Listen. This airplane phone is terrible. Do me a favor and tell Paige that I'll call her about tomorrow's breakfast when I land."

"Will do," said Thad.

I bolted out of my chair.

"Gotta run, Thad. Late for something."

I raced down the hall, forgetting about my newly nagging meniscus, and grabbed Jake from his cubicle outside Thad's office.

"Come here, now."

He dutifully followed me to a copy room. Just out of college, he looked puzzled and frightened at once. We had had no significant relationship before this moment.

"Ummm, what's up?" he asked.

"Do you want a month of free lunches?"

He shifted back a step.

"Yeah, I guess. But this isn't like...sexual or something."

"No, no, no. Just do me a favor. If Thad asks you if I told you not to invite me to the Audi meeting, tell him I didn't. Can you do that? I'll load up your cafeteria card for a month."

"Cash is cool too," said Jake.

"Fine. I'll give you two hundred dollars."

He leaned casually against a copier.

"I see myself spending at least four hundred a month in the café."

"I'll give you three hundred."

"OK. And you're telling me that all I have to do is tell Thad you told me not to invite you to the meeting."

I resisted the urge to call him a moron.

"No, tell him that I *did not* tell you. You don't even remember who I am."

"Oh, so it will be my screw-up then?"

"Well, yeah, I suppose. Just say that you accidentally skipped my name among the people you were supposed to invite. OK?"

"That'll cost you four hundred."

"Fine. Four hundred. Just do it."

I waited a few minutes after Jake left the copy room. My phone vibrated repeatedly with messages from John, who was no doubt wondering what was taking me so long. As I exited, I glanced over at Jake's cubicle. Thad was standing over him, doling out punishment. Jake was nodding his head and taking it. Perfect.

I ran and got my bag, noting briefly that I was behaving like a crazy person. But then I told myself it was all Thad's fault. What an asshole.

Fuck him, as usual.

* * * *

WHEN I GOT BACK to the restaurant, John was morose. Before I could apologize, I picked up my Margarita and guzzled it down. All of the ice had melted. It tasted more of lime water and salt than tequila. I poured another.

"Change of plans," said John. "Fucking Simon is coming back early. I have to meet him at five to write a speech for him. I'll be working all night."

"Shit. That sucks."

"And he's been drinking on the plane. He's an asshole when he's drunk. Completely unfocused and self-pitying."

He took a sip of the Corona he had switched to and smiled wryly.

"The man is leading a major media company and drinking on the job. Totally unprofessional."

"Did you cancel with your girlfriends?" I asked.

"Yeah, we'll do it another time. But stop by my office after I see Simon. I have a bottle of Johnnie Walker Blue. Maybe I'll ask Jennie to come down."

"Sure. What the hell."

Diane would be returning from Puerto Rico in roughly 48 hours. I had pretty much decided to drink my way through the majority of them. We headed back to the building, went through our usual drunken express elevator machinations, and returned to our respective offices.

Lily shook her head as I passed.

"What in God's name are you doing, Paul?"

"I'm not here," I said.

I shut the door and called my mother. I hoped she was out

taking Aidan for an afternoon walk.

"Come on, come on, answering machine, please."

Bingo. I left her a rambling message about how I was being forced to attend a launch event sponsored by a big client. All hands on deck. I told her I would leave work early on Tuesday to pick Aidan up. I felt OK with the whole thing because my mother had a crib at her house too. She was used to this, and Aidan would obviously be in better hands than mine. Diane would find out, of course, but I figured I would just use the same lie on her.

I hung up, lowered the lights, and took a nap.

* * * *

I WAS AWAKENED BY A CALL from John at 6:30 PM.

"Come on up," he said.

I grunted an OK and looked for my jacket. It didn't look much worse than it had earlier because I had laid it down neatly on the floor to avoid additional wrinkles. My pants, on the other hand, were bunched up in the front. As I attempted to smooth them out, I noticed a salsa stain above the right knee. I poured some bottled water on a napkin and scrubbed as best I could.

I peeked out my door and took in a dead-quiet office. With Mitch away, the staff had clearly taken the opportunity to bolt at a decent hour. I felt a sheet of paper under my foot and picked it up. Someone had slid a note under my door. Paige's handwriting: *Please leave me your beach ball. I really need it!*

"Again with the fucking beach ball," I said.

Mine was at home, in Aidan's crib. I took a tour around the office in hopes of finding an extra one, but quickly began losing hope. Given how aggressively Paige had been retrieving them, what were the odds? I passed by the fish bowl and headed down a long corridor leading to our finance department. Then I had a thought: the finance people. Jessica, the director, and her two associates, Mary Ellen and Dabney, sat in an off-the-beaten-path nook in the floor's northwest corner. Jessica had a cramped windowless office, Dabney had a cubicle right outside of it, and Mary Ellen had a larger cubicle set further back. Unlike most cubicles, Mary Ellen's had some privacy, with taller walls that nearly reached the ceiling. I had no idea why. It's not like the finance people sat around counting large stacks of cash. But none of that was important. What was important was that Mary Ellen had just recently gone on maternity leave. Her workspace was so remote... Might Paige have forgotten to check there for a beach ball? I was fairly sure the balls had originally been distributed by our mail clerk, so he probably would have dropped one on Mary Ellen's desk by rote.

I quietly entered the department, feeling slightly ridiculous but exhilarated. It was clear from Jessica's closed door and darkened office that she and Dabney had both gone home. I walked slowly to Mary Ellen's cubicle and looked in.

Her in-box was empty but for one thing: a beach ball.

I picked it up with two hands and sat down at Mary Ellen's desk. I leaned back in her chair and closed my eyes for a few seconds. When I opened them, I casually surveyed the desk. It was impeccably neat. A desk organizer contained five identical felt tip pens, five new Carlyle Nash pencils, gold paper clips, silver small binder clips, a sticky note dispenser and a faux diamond-encrusted letter opener. To the right of the computer monitor sat a wedding photo. Mary Ellen was no great beauty and her husband, unsurprisingly, was no Brad Pitt. I leaned in for a closer look. He looked familiar, but I couldn't quite place his thirtyish, nebbishy face. Perhaps I had seen him in the building. Perhaps elsewhere. A research vendor maybe? Whatever the case, I thought, their baby wouldn't have a modeling career in its future.

I stood up and pushed the chair back, making sure to place it exactly as it had been positioned. A mild paranoia arose as I did so. Stealing a five-cent beach ball wasn't exactly the crime of the century, but I was nonetheless doing something vaguely dishonest. My mind began to race.

Holy shit. There are security cameras in the hallway. What if security has been watching me this whole time? What if they're watching me this very second? What if two hulking fucking mouth-breathers are on their way up?

I looked up at the ceiling and saw that there were no additional cameras in this secluded corner of the office. I took three long breaths to calm down. To be safe, I would have to hide the beach ball for the trip down the monitored hallway. I quickly unplugged the spout and released the air. As I squeezed the last bit out, the ball virtually disappeared in my clenched fist, but the incentive card was still firmly affixed to it. As it flopped over the back of my hand, my focus shifted to the bold-faced 150 ad-page target. And at that moment, everything clicked.

Mitch doesn't care about the beach balls at all! He only cares about getting the incentive cards back!

I began connecting the dots. He had issued the incentive because he'd been worried about meeting Issue Number Two's ad-page goal. He had then recalled it immediately because Friday's PR shit storm had been much, much worse than he had imagined it might be. Caught in a constant cycle of managing his messaging to the Lou Lamonts of the media world, there was no way he could let it leak that he had set an embarrassingly bullish ad projection for Issue Number Two. With *World* bleeding booked pages, I knew that Mitch's new PR goal would be to convey that a lighter, thinner magazine was exactly what he had planned following the colossal record-breaking launch issue. I could practically script his pitch myself: *Come on, Lou. We've always envisioned World as an exclusive advertising environment. Issue One was a big party that everyone wanted in on. That's why it was so thick. Maybe even too thick. But sixty-five to seventy-five ad pages is truly the range we expect and, quite frankly, the magazine we want to be.*

If someone like Lou Lamont knew about the beach ball and incentive card, *that* would be the PR shit storm of the century.

The product-recall story was a lie. But it was the only way to get everyone on staff to return the incentive cards without drawing attention to the fact that Mitch was lowering *World's* ad-page goals. At tomorrow's breakfast, he would no doubt spin the staff the same way he would try to spin the trades—and all to protect his heretofore unblemished reputation. Lesser publishers might fall short of ad goals, but not the great Mitch Blake. No way, no how.

"Prediction," I whispered. "He's going to give the entire staff a day off no matter what. This way no one gives another thought to the incentive card. It never even happened."

I realized that I was pacing like a madman, so I stopped and took another deep breath. I shoved the deflated beach ball down the back of my pants and walked out as casually as possible. Midway down the corridor I spotted the security camera, encased in a black dome about the size of half a cantaloupe. I walked at a normal pace, with nothing in my happily swinging hands, and never looking up.

I went directly to Paige's office and scrawled, "Here's your stupid beach ball" on a sticky note. I reinflated the ball and left it on her chair...but I would test my theory.

I kept the incentive card. ▪

CHAPTER EIGHT

Bellwether Games
(2005)

DIANE BELIEVED there was a cosmic reason the only thing the previous owners of our house left behind was an egg timer. She had found it in the back of a kitchen cabinet two days after we moved in. Although it was stained and a bit sticky, she had called it a gift. She wound it up now and set it in front of me.

"You have five minutes to talk about *Bellwether*."

"OK, fine. Should I cc Michael when I send the 'Brains Are Back' one-sheet to Mitch?"

"Why is that important?" she asked as she unpacked coffee mugs.

"Because he's my boss. I know Mitch asked me to do it directly, but I don't want Michael to think I'm going behind his back or something. Am I overthinking it?"

"Oh, no. Of course not, Paul. You never overthink anything."

I picked up the egg timer and reset it.

"New rule. Every time you say something sarcastic, the timer goes back to five minutes."

"Then you should probably hold the timer."

I reset it again.

"So," I said slowly, "should I cc Michael when I send the one-sheet to Mitch?"

"No, you should not."

"Why not?"

"Paul…all you ever do is complain about hierarchy and the layers between you and your false idol—excuse me, Mitch. Now, at your first opportunity to bypass all that, you want to cc Michael because you want to be a good boy."

I nodded.

"You're right. You're right. I won't cc him."

"I'm always right, Paul."

She picked up the egg timer and turned it to zero. It rang.

"What are we doing for dinner?" she asked.

* * * *

I PROOFED THE ONE-SHEET OVER AND OVER on my train ride in, scribbling and erasing furiously in the margins as I sat crammed between a pair of fellow commuters. As we pulled into Penn Station, the familiar white-haired Wall Street veteran to my right smiled and said he would bring me a new pencil the next day.

I reached the office at 7:40 AM and made my edits to the copy. I then transferred the write-up into our standard one-sheet template with the *Bellwether* logo in the lower right and the 'Brains Are Back' tagline in the lower left. I read the piece yet again and felt good about it. It was well written, and I had added some new "smart" supporting facts: museum visits were at an all-time high, book readings were the hottest events in Manhattan, PBS ratings were way up… If there was anything I demanded from my own work it was that it be original. In my short time at the magazine, I had become obsessed with putting my own personal stamp on projects. This was something that Michael didn't necessarily do. And while I didn't dislike him, he was no John Steffans, who, despite his love of leisure and liquor, could write circles around most everyone I had worked with to that point.

As my colleagues started showing up and settling in at their desks, I realized I was still reading. It was already 8:40. I wrote my email:

Hello, Mitch: Attached please find the positioning one-sheet you requested yesterday. If you have any questions, comments, or edits, please let me know. Thanks, Paul

As I hit *send*, Sam Martz, a marketing contemporary, entered backwards in his rolling chair from his office next door. Sam was a good guy but living proof that virtually anyone could get rehired at Carlyle Nash. He had been forced out at two sister magazines for lack of productivity, but he had a remarkable ability to ace interviews and leverage his personal networks. Michael had recently been all over him for projects he had been ignoring.

"What's up, man?" he asked as he grabbed a stress ball from my desk and tossed it against a wall.

"Same old shit," I answered. "What's up with you?"

"Well, I've got some news. I'm out of here."

I feigned surprise, sure that he had been fired again.

"Shit, Sam. You're kidding me? What happened?"

He put his feet up on my table.

"I'm leaving for Jessup and Greer. I nabbed the top marketing spot at *Modern Parent*."

I was stunned but tried to hide it. Jessup & Greer was one of Carlyle Nash's largest competitors, and *Modern Parent* was the childcare category leader. It was a big job, and I feared Sam would be in over his head. Or rather, I knew Sam would be in over his head. Actual work was always a major inconvenience for him.

"Wow," I said. "That's incredible, Sam. Congrats."

"Thanks, man. It was just time, you know? I need a bigger challenge."

I had to take a call from a sales rep, so I wished him luck and he rolled back out. On a practical level, his announcement was good news because his eventual replacement would immediately be handling a bigger share of our department workload than Sam had been. But how the heck had he pulled it off?

I looked at my watch and realized that I had forgotten to call Diane at 8:15, as promised. She had asked me to check my office files for some benefits information she needed before she left for work. I dialed her cell phone to apologize but got her voicemail. I left the usual self-flagellating apology, but I didn't give my transgression much more thought after hanging up. She would have to understand.

I was working on a Buick presentation for our Detroit office when Mitch's email response arrived. I excitedly opened it, expecting a "Great job, Paul!" and was disappointed to read only "Please drop off a hard copy. Will take a look."

I feared for a moment that I had breached protocol by sending the document as an email but was confident enough in the quality of what I had produced to think that he would forgive the mistake. I printed a copy and ran it down the hall to his assistant. I returned to my office and waited nervously, picking up the stress ball and digging my nails in to see how long it would take for the marks to disappear. I knew Mitch wanted to move quickly on the one-sheet, but I was prepared for at least a few edits. I tried to get back to the Buick presentation but found myself instead just watching my email. I switched the stress ball to my other hand.

I saw the subject line of the message first: *'BRAINS ARE BACK' ONE-SHEET*. But as I sat up in my chair, I saw that it was from Lois Knight, *Bellwether's* Ad Director, and was addressed to our individual sales reps, with Mitch and Marketing-All cc'd. It simply read:

See attached for a new brand positioning one-sheet. Mitch will discuss in today's sales-only meeting. —LK

I opened the attachment to see if any changes had been made to my draft. There were none. But despite the fact I had delivered a document that Mitch apparently deemed perfect, I was disappointed. Not a single word of acknowledgement? On the other hand, I did admire the way he had expeditiously moved the sheet along so the reps could use it. No red tape in Mitch's world.

I dialed Diane to vent but again got her voicemail. I hung up, sat back, and watched my email for a few minutes. Nothing. I shook my head and started to work. Once I got deep into the Buick presentation, the day flew by. After wrapping up a few smaller quick turnaround items, I was in good shape by 4:30. I realized I had never eaten lunch, so I grabbed a few singles from my wallet and headed down to the vending machine in the pantry. It was at the end of a long hallway decorated with covers of *Bellwether* dating back to the 1920s. About a third of the way down, I saw Mitch emerge from the pantry, tearing open a bag of trail mix and pouring it into his mouth. *Here we go*, I thought. At long last, I'd hear the "Hey, great job" I'd been pining for. The gap closed between us and I raised my hand.

"Hi, Mitch."

He was chewing, but I heard him clearly as he passed in a blur.

"Jessup and Greer? I don't know. They're losing market share. But good luck over there."

I stopped dead in my tracks and turned, but he was already 10 yards past and not breaking stride.

"But I, but, that's not, um…OK. Thanks. Thanks Mitch."

As I plodded to the pantry, head spinning, all I could think was *What the hell was that?* I may have even said the words aloud as I walked up to the vending machine and stood blankly before it. Had he really just mistaken me for the departing Sam? Fucking Sam? The guy who practically floated through the office? For God's sake, I had just been in Mitch's office the day before! I had handled an important assignment flawlessly. He had seen my name on several recent group emails praising my work…hadn't he? But now he was attaching Sam's name to my face? Impossible.

Or wait a minute. I get it. He's just messing with me. It's one big mind fuck. He knows me. He knows I nailed the one-sheet. But he doesn't want me to get too cocky. Is that it? What kind of sick bastard does that? No, that can't be it. Maybe he did just mix me up with Sam. He barely looked me in the eye when I was in his office. But is that worse? What the fuck?

"Are you going to make a selection?" asked a voice from behind.

I swung around to see an intern with a dollar in his hand waiting to use the vending machine.

"Yes…no," I said. "Just go ahead."

I headed back to my office and called Diane. Voicemail again. Where the hell was she when I needed to talk? ▪

CHAPTER NINE

Captain *World*
(2007)

I T WASN'T UNTIL John turned on his speakerphone that I came to.

"Captain *World*," the female voice cooed. "Captain *Woooorld*. Wake up, Captain *World*."

"Alright, good, he's waking up," said John.

"Morning, sunshine," said the cheerful voice. "Did we have fun last night or what?"

I unfolded from my fetal position on John's form-over-function office couch, which was backless, s-shaped, and hard as slate. I lifted my head and discovered that I had used my balled-up jacket as a pillow. It was wet with drool. I was wearing only a t-shirt, briefs and black socks. My dress shirt, tie, and slacks were draped over a chair. I sat up, slowly lowered my feet to the floor, and groaned. A painful rhythmic thump reverberated through my head. My first hazy thought was that I needed to warm up a morning bottle for Aidan, but then I remembered where I was. John watched me from behind his desk. An empty bottle of Johnnie Walker Blue sat within reach on my side of his desktop. I reflexively looked to see if the office door was shut. It was. A battered red-white-and-blue kite with a mass of tangled string hung on a hook on the back of the door.

"I'll talk to you later," said John. "He's completely out of it. Give me a heads-up when Simon gets in."

"Awwww, I want to talk to the captain," the female voice said.

"Believe me, you don't."

John hung up.

"What the hell is going on?" I asked.

John picked up the bottle and waggled it from side to side.

"Hellooooo? Remember me?"

"Oh man. I think I remember the first glass, maybe. How much did I drink?"

"You drank the whole thing with Jennie while I worked on Simon's speech. You owe me. Do you know how much this shit costs? Madelyn gave it to me for our anniversary."

"I'm sorry. I don't know how—"

John gave me a pitying look. "Blank memory? And please put your pants on before you answer."

I stepped gingerly to the chair and started dressing.

"I don't know. The beach ball and then…"

"Beach ball? What beach ball?"

"Nothing, nothing. I vaguely remember some girl wearing a beret."

John took a bottled water from his fridge and handed it to me.

"There was a girl, alright. Jennie. Simon's assistant. But I don't know anything about a beret."

I shook my head and sat down.

"How can you not remember? You flew a kite with her!"

"We flew a kite? At night? In the city?"

John crossed to the door and gathered up the kite. He walked back and dropped it at my feet.

"I don't know if it flew," he said, "but the two of you came back here at midnight laughing like idiots. It's a miracle I got the speech done."

"Why was she calling me Captain something?"

"She said you went on this rant about how Mitch wouldn't have been able to launch *World* without you and how you had something that would make him stop underestimating you. I didn't get all the details. At some point, you apparently started calling yourself Captain *World*. Sounds to me like you were a complete asshole. But Jennie thought you were a riot."

I covered my face with my hands.

"Did I do anything with her? I've got all I can handle right now."

"No. You were a good boy. Even if it had gotten to that, you could barely function. You were gone. She took off when you started singing some song your mother sang to you as a baby. That was just weird. But, hey, you made a new friend."

"Please don't let her see me again," I said as I tied my shoes. The room spun as I straightened up. I reached for my jacket and unballed it. It was unwearable. There wouldn't, couldn't, be a day three for it.

"Oh no," I said. "Look at this thing."

John crossed to his closet, took out a brown herringbone blazer, and tossed it to me.

"This should go with your pants," he said. "Wear it once and get it fucking dry cleaned before you bring it back."

I put it on. It was just slightly short in the sleeves and a bit loose in the middle, but it would do.

"Thanks," I said as I looked at my watch.

It was 7:45, so at least I would appear to be a morning go-getter when I arrived at *World*. I looked around and didn't see my bag, then remembered I'd left it in my office.

"Lunch today?" asked John.

"Hell no. Mitch is back and I have to leave early to pick up Aidan. *Do not* call me. I am drying out."

"Alright. I'll call you tomorrow."

The stairwell was just outside John's office and presented the best way to avoid running into Jennie. Even though I could just barely remember her face, she would surely remember Captain *World*'s.

You're such an asshole.

I emerged out of breath on the *World* floor and headed straight to the men's room. I looked like hell. My dark brown hair, which I normally wore parted conservatively to the side, was a mess. I wet it down and slicked it back, which made me look untrustworthy. But I kind of liked it. My eyes were red, so I figured I would put on the low prescription glasses I kept in my bag. If anyone asked why I was wearing them, I'd say my allergies were acting up. With the slicked-back hair and the herringbone jacket, the glasses would round out a decidedly different look.

Back at my desk, I breathed a sigh of relief when I saw my bag where I'd left it. I found the glasses, put them on, and looked at my reflection in a small mirror hung on my bulletin board. I stroked my one-day stubble as I admired the look. Kind of sharp. Captain *World* indeed. I grabbed a travel size can of hairspray from a drawer and froze the style in place.

I checked email and saw one from Paige with the subject line *Here we go again...* It was a link to an article from a media gossip website called Gape.com. They had had it in for *World* from the very beginning. It purported to be a behind-the-scenes account of backstabbing and dysfunction on our editorial side. It sounded entirely accurate—right down to Jimmy Stillman's contractually agreed-upon body waxings and French tutor. But at least there was no mention of any troubles on the business side. Mitch probably sent them pizzas and a masseuse every day at noon.

The next email down was a staff reminder about the team breakfast. It would be starting a bit late, at 9:30, because Mitch had flown in on a red-eye—which kind of made two of us. I called home to check the answering machine. There were two messages from the night before. The first was from Diane:

"I spoke to your mother. You're incredible, Paul. I'm thrilled she's watching Aidan, but I would love to know what was so important that you had to dump him for the entire night. Don't tell me. Mitch needed his coffee warmed up or his car washed. Please tell me you're still taking off Tuesday for the pediatrician. If you canceled the appointment, I swear I will kill you. Call me at the hotel or on my cell in the morning. I have to give you my flight details for tomorrow. I'm not leaving them on an answering machine. You might spill your beer hitting the playback button. Bye."

"I love you too," I said.

The second message had come from out of the blue. Our old landlord, Keith, who I hadn't seen in a few years, said that a letter had arrived for me at our former Hicksville address. He read off the name on the return address. It was an old friend from my Florida days, someone I had worked with at *Blowback*. Keith said he would hold onto it for me. He signed off by telling me to "Rock on," and I felt a pang of nostalgia for those simpler times with Diane. I made a mental note to pick up the letter when I had the chance.

* * * *

WHEN I ARRIVED for the breakfast meeting in the large, already-crowded conference room, one of Paige's junior staffers—smiling like a flight attendant—handed me a deep tan envelope sealed with an orange sunburst reading *DON'T OPEN YET*. I surveyed the standing-room only crowd and saw that everyone was holding one. Younger staffers were tittering with anticipation. An older staffer standing near me muttered that it was probably just a discount card from an advertiser. I, on the other hand, was pretty sure I knew what was inside: an announcement of a diversionary day off from our benevolent leader. I rapped the envelope excitedly against my knuckles in anticipation of triumphant confirmation of my deduction. Across a conference table decked out with bagels, Danish, and breakfast fruit, I caught sight of a junior staffer eyeing me warily. I stopped hitting myself with the envelope just as she turned quickly away. A coffee urn was at the far end of the table, so I snaked my way toward it through the crowd.

"Hey, Paul," said Antonio from the art department. "Liking the new look."

"Thanks, Antonio," I said as I shook his hand.

"Slick, Paul," said Karl from production.

Karl slapped me on the shoulder as I passed. The pain in my head flowed from back to front, then back again. My right ear popped, increasing the volume of the room from loud to blaring.

"Thanks, Karl. I'm gonna press charges for that."

Lily, always the wallflower at staff gatherings, was standing in a corner, picking at a small plate of fruit. I prepared a cup of coffee with more milk than usual, chugged it down, and poured another. There was room next to Lily so I squeezed in, leaned my head against the wall, and moaned softly. She elbowed me.

"You do know I have your best interests at heart, right?"

"Not necessarily," I answered, "but go ahead."

"You look ridiculous. And where did you get that jacket?"

"This? I bought it. You've seen it before."

She reached for my lapel and felt the fabric.

"No, Paul, I haven't. And you never buy anything."

"Well, I bought this jacket," I said as I took a grape from her plate. "And a little image shake-up never harmed anyone."

Paige approached.

"I got it, thanks," she said, obviously referring to the beach ball. "Charming note too, but I also need the—"

"Mitch is here," said Lily.

All three of us turned our attention to Mitch making his entrance, glad-handing sales reps on his way in. His arrival in any room always had a magnetic north effect of shutting down individual conversations. Nevertheless, I tugged at Paige's sleeve and leaned in close.

"I know," I said. "You need the incentive card too. Am I right?"

"Yes. Mitch wants everything back. Even though only the beach ball was recalled, he wants to play it safe. I know...it's crazy...but he's the boss."

"OK. No problem. I found it on the floor of my office. It must have fallen off. I'll give it to you right after this."

I had my proof. Mitch had indeed told Paige to make sure the cards were returned with the beach balls. That she herself appeared to have no inkling of Mitch's true intent was, I thought, intellectually damning. In fact, I was by all indications the only person who had figured out what Mitch was thinking. I didn't know that for a fact, of course, but as I scanned the faces in the room to see if there was anyone with at least a furrowed brow, all I saw was juvenile giddiness and veteran boredom. How could that be? Why wasn't it obvious to everyone that the product-recall story was bull? I had once thought of these people as the best of the best by mere virtue of the fact that Mitch had hired them. Now I viewed them with pity and scorn. They were morons, all of them. Just like that, I had gone from believing that nearly everyone at *World*—except Thad—was a level above the typical Carlyle Nasher to realizing that only I could match wits with Mitch, and only I could peel back his layers to reveal a core of perpetual plotting and deception. Mitch might be two steps ahead of everyone else, but not me. I was a goddamn genius. I grabbed a raspberry Danish from the table and devoured it in three bites. The junior staffer was eyeing me again. What was her fucking problem?

Thad had entered the room right on Mitch's heels. He did this constantly to remind everyone that he was Mitch's second-in-command and make it look like they had just finished a piece of important private business. It was pathetic. In reality, he probably had followed Mitch into and out of the men's room, and handed him a hand towel after he washed up. I fantasized throwing a pumpernickel bagel at his face with enough force to break his nose and then cutting through the frenzied, cheering crowd and pouring hot coffee on his bloodied face. He clapped his hands together like a Kindergarten teacher.

"Your attention please!" he shouted. "Let's welcome Mitch back from San Francisco. I know he has some big news for us. Mitch..."

"Thanks," said Mitch as he adjusted a cufflink. "And good morning, everyone. I don't *really* have big news for you. I just wanted to get everyone together to tell you how much I appreciate your hard work. I know we hit a little speed bump the other day, but it's truly nothing I'm worried about. I've always told you that people would be sniping at *World*. But hey, that comes with the territory when you do something big, bold, and ambitious. I don't care what anyone says. Jimmy and his team put together a great first issue, and we don't need any ink-stained critic to tell us what he thought of it—bad or good—to know that *World* will not just remake the general-interest category but become the singular magazine of its generation."

Mitch paused as Thad handed him a glass of orange juice. As he took a sip, his eyes fell on me for not more than a second. A fleeting, barely perceptible look of surprise crossed his face as he took in my new look. He set down his glass.

"On the flight back," he continued, "I read a great quote from none other than Bill Gates. Here's what he said: 'To create a new standard it takes something that's not just a little bit different. It takes something that's really new and really captures people's imaginations.' Don't ever forget that this is precisely what we've done here. *World* Magazine made the biggest thunk in industry history. Now open those envelopes...because I lied. There is big news."

I tore open mine as quickly as anyone around me. The card read simply:

SUMMER ACHIEVEMENT AWARD
WORLD OFFICE CLOSED THIS THURSDAY AND FRIDAY
ENJOY!

Motherfucker. He gave us two days off.

As my colleagues whooped and hollered in thanks and adoration, I pounded my fist into my thigh. I was disappointed that I hadn't predicted the move with perfect accuracy. I should have known Mitch would go the grand-gesture route. This act of unprecedented corporate generosity would surely make everyone forget that there had ever been a beach ball, and certainly that there had ever been a paging incentive. It was brilliant. Lily and Paige bounced up and down to my right. Paige was speaking to me but I could only see her lips moving in slow motion.

"Caaaaan youuuuuu beeelieeeeve thiiiiiissss?" she seemed to be saying.

Everything, in fact, seemed to have slowed down as in a dream. To my left, Antonio climbed atop a chair.

"Thank you, Mitch!" he screamed.

My ears rang, my head pounded, time speeded up, and I could hear again.

"You're welcome, you're welcome," said Mitch.

The room calmed in an instant as he raised his hands and then lowered them.

"Enjoy it, folks. We are on the brink of some big wins and celebrating a couple of West Coast victories. The San Francisco office turned around a huge one yesterday with Providence Insurance, and I'm certain there are more to come. Let's get to work."

As he made his exit to an Antonio-led chant of "Mitch! Mitch! Mitch!" I fumed. How could he not credit me publicly for the Providence turnaround? My paper must have been critical to changing their minds. But not even a word of thanks from Mitch.

"Fucking bullshit," I muttered as I crushed my coffee cup and tossed it to the table.

"Ummmm, Paul?" said Lily. "Why are you the only unhappy person in this room?"

"I don't know, Lily. I thought we were all getting ponies." ▪

CHAPTER TEN

The *Bellwether* Woman
(2005)

THE THEME OF *BELLWETHER'S* 2005 National Sales Meeting was "The Final Lap." Closing in on profitability for the first time in decades, the revitalized magazine had been defying expectations thanks to a smart new editor named Henry Wallace and Mitch's business leadership. Our "Brains Are Back" brand positioning had succeeded in attracting the most diverse lineup of advertisers of all the magazines in the Carlyle Nash stable: from John Hancock to Jack Daniels, from Lufthansa to Lean Cuisine. Everyone wanted in. *Bellwether* was a juggernaut.

The national sales meeting featured a jam-packed agenda designed to set the team's sights on moving the magazine back into the black once and for all. The two-day conference included everything from team-building exercises to sales role-play to motivational speakers to Q&A sessions with editors and star writers. Under the magazine's previous leadership—and even now at other Carlyle Nash titles—sales meetings were merely an annual excuse to stay at a five-star hotel, get drunk on the Moreland family's tab, and maybe cheat on your spouse. But things were different under Mitch. Although we were booked into an appropriately fabulous Midtown hotel, it might as well have been Riker's Island. The printed agenda elicited audible moans from the people in my department when it landed in our in-boxes a week before the conference. Day One: Breakfast at 6:30 AM. Opening Remarks at 7:00. Sales Boot Camp, Part 1 of 8 at 7:45... Staffers murmured that labor laws were being broken.

I was perfectly fine with it.

In the roughly six months since Mitch had mistaken me for Sam Martz, I had become relentlessly focused. He wasn't going to mistake me for someone else ever again. I continued to produce strong work for both of the sales reps I assisted directly, as well as for Michael and other members of the marketing department. However, the structural dynamic remained unchanged: Michael was our nominal department head and, as such, was ensconced in Mitch's inner circle. I could only hope that the persistent rumors of Michael being up for a VP spot at Jessup & Greer were true. But there was no way of knowing. Each evening, I would complain to Diane about my frustrating dearth of recognition and face time with Mitch. The egg timer was getting a workout.

The first page of the program featured a custom-designed logo of a checkered flag with the words "The Final Lap" printed below. I excitedly flipped to the second page and ran my finger down over the raised lettering to the 2:45-3:00 PM time slot on Day Two. Topic: Marketing Presentation for *Bellwether*'s First Annual Sports Issue. Presenter: Paul Cavanaugh. This, at long last, would be my chance to shine. Fifteen minutes to make clear to Mitch and the entire team that the guy in the windowless office could bring it, with substance and wit...like my Uncle Frank taught me.

When I was a kid, the most frequent visitor to the house

was Francis Cavanaugh, my father's youngest brother. If Dad had been the rock-solid husband and dutiful provider until his sudden death of a heart attack at age 64, Uncle Frank had always been the opposite. Single and happy, free of stress, he still showed up armed with a thousand stories and a limitless supply of jokes. Comic timing, he always said, was the world's most underrated talent. *If you've got it, put it at the top of your résumé.* By the time I was five, he already had me performing jokes for him. If I stammered, he stopped me. If I didn't hold a pause long enough, he'd rub out his cigarette and take me through the paces properly. When my mother inevitably shouted from the kitchen that I had homework to do, he would fire back that the ability to hold an audience was way more important than times tables. She would remind him that he was an insurance broker, not Jack Benny.

"Not for long, Agnes," he would say. "I'm going on the road soon. Now go back to poisoning my brother."

As I set pen to paper to prepare my presentation, Uncle Frank's advice came back to me. The nonverbals first: casually button your blazer just before you reach the podium; adjust the mike gently like you've done it a million times before; look at the back row first; smile. I wrote those instructions down first and then went through a dozen variations of an opening remark.

The words themselves, or my ability to string them together, came from my father. Uncle Frank may have known how to entertain, but Dad knew how to write. For 30-plus years he worked in corporate communications for American Express, pumping out press releases, CEO speeches, corporate bios and briefings. Even after a long day and a long commute, he'd sit down at the kitchen table and start filling up page after page of a legal pad. I'd watch him concentrate and think that whatever he was writing down had to be really important and wonder if maybe I'd get to do the same kind of work someday.

* * * *

IN ITS LONG HISTORY, *BELLWETHER* had never devoted an entire issue to the subject of sports, but Henry Wallace was a fan. He also wanted to pay tribute to the magazine's overlooked history of reporting on baseball, boxing, and golf. I set out to deliver a presentation that could be used to overcome any disconnect among potential advertisers while also showing our sales staff that the magazine's occasional sports coverage was indeed superior to typical sports writing. I was a fan too, so I felt I was the right man for the job.

I dug deep into the magazine's archives and worked late for five straight days before the meeting. Diane was patient with the process, muting the late local news to let me rehearse to her each night. She was excited for me too, but mostly just happy that I wasn't complaining for once. By the final evening, however, she was done.

"Paul...please, it's perfect. You're ready. You'll do great."

"Just one more time, Diane. I swear. Minor word change on slide nine."

But she was right. I was ready.

Nevertheless, I could barely pay attention to the Day One presentations—sneaking peaks at my index cards every few minutes and rehearsing over and over in my head. Only during the first night's dinner, when even Mitch relaxed for a few minutes to sip an Amstel Light, did I power down.

Each table was anchored, so to speak, by a member of our management team. I was pleased to be at Michael's table because I didn't have to kiss up to him. As bosses went, he was mellow and pretty low-maintenance—which I chalked up to a peace of mind that came from delegating everything that landed on his desk. I was seated between Joyce Duncan, our Southeast Territory rep, and Emily Frazier, one of *Bellwether's* star writers and special editorial guests. It was an interesting combination because Emily was a London-based Rhodes Scholar and intrepid

Middle East reporter while Joyce thought Yasser Arafat was the name of a night cream. Emily had deep contacts in U.S. Intelligence and the Saudi Arabian government; Joyce had valuable access to Miami media buyers who liked being treated to day spa visits and South Beach lunches.

"It's soooo nice to meet you, Emily," Joyce screeched across me.

"A pleasure," said Emily in a clipped British accent.

"I just love, love, love your writing."

"Thank you."

Speaking to a top writer without acknowledging the existence of the marketing guy sitting between you was actually pretty typical for a sales rep. Only when I leaned forward for a piece of bread did Joyce acknowledge me...by gently pushing me back to an upright position.

"Sorry, Peter, I couldn't see Emily."

"It's OK. I don't need to eat. And you can call me Paul."

I glanced at Emily and she smiled.

"Whatever you like, sweetie," said Joyce. "So Emily...I thought your Tony Blair profile was genius."

"Yes," said Emily. "It really was ingenious. I only wish I'd written it."

"Excuse me?" said Joyce. "You mean someone wrote it for you?"

Emily tapped my forearm.

"So what do you do at *Bellwether*, Paul?"

"Me? Oh I work in marketing. You know...presentations, research, copywriting."

"Peter is great," said Joyce. "Really great."

"Thanks, Joan," I said. "I think you're fantastic too."

Emily pushed her seat back and turned toward me so that I was directly obstructing Joyce's sight line. As annoying as Joyce was, I felt bad that I was effectively being used to block her from the conversation. But as Emily slowly crossed her bare legs and locked her gaze upon me, I shifted her way. I knew Joyce was getting the message behind me when I heard her ask the person to her right if she was using the wrong bread plate.

Emily was prettier from the front than from the side. She had what I would call a writerly sort of beauty. Short, unfussy brown hair, just a touch of makeup, and the attractive air of someone who does what they love for a living. I gripped my dinner napkin tightly in fear, knowing I was not as educated and informed as she was. She reached to the table for her red wine, leaned back, and took a sip.

"Tell me about these presentations you do, Paul."

"It's Peter," I said with a smile.

She laughed. The room felt warmer so I took off my navy blue blazer and slung it over the back of my chair. I was wearing a peach polo shirt that I always thought made my arms look good.

"You do look like a Peter, you know. Or maybe John. Something biblical and Irish."

"How do you know I'm Irish?"

She gestured to my place card.

"I assumed Cavanaugh isn't Russian…"

I picked up the place card and laughed.

"…and you have freckles on your arms," she added.

"Oh, these. I had them done."

"Do give me your surgeon's name," she countered. "They're adorable."

We bantered on for some time until I asked her about a recent article she had written on women in Afghanistan. She seemed impressed by some of the details I recalled, and I otherwise nodded in all the right places. She had a way of putting me at ease.

After a brief pause in our conversation, she touched my forearm lightly and smiled.

"I like you, Paul Cavanaugh."

My skin tingled. I smiled back as she looked over my shoulder.

"I see I'm not the only special guest at the table," she said.

I turned and looked. Taking a seat was a man to whom I'd never been introduced but recognized immediately. It was John's boss, the infamous Simon Bell.

I had heard that he would be appearing on the next day's leadership panel with three other Carlyle Nash senior executives, but I hadn't expected him at the first night's dinner. I wasn't surprised that he wasn't seated at Mitch's table, given the rumors of friction and rivalry between the two men.

Before saying hello to any of us, Simon motioned to a waiter.

"Mate," he said in his Australian accent, "would you be so kind as to bring me a Tanqueray and tonic?"

Simon's genteel way of speaking seemed at odds with his rugged look. Bearded and thick-armed, he looked like a man who would be at home on a cattle ranch—the rough opposite of Mitch's blond coastal cool.

Joyce could hardly contain herself.

"Hi, Simon!" she yelled across the table.

"Joyce Duncan," said Simon. "How long has it been?"

His eyes shifted to me and Emily as Joyce answered, "A whole year, Simon!" They lingered on Emily for more than a second. She held his stare, and I felt an odd sense of possessiveness as Simon gaze-groped the woman who had seemed to be flirting with me. But just as quickly my envy turned to marital guilt. I reached into a pants pocket and felt for the note Diane had slipped into my briefcase before the conference: *You are ready. You will be great. I love you.*

"You look familiar, mate" said Simon. "Did you work for me at *Gloss*?"

I didn't realize Simon was talking to me. Thinking about Diane's note reminded me not only that I loved my wife but also that I had a presentation to give the next day. I reflexively reached into the opposite pants pocket to make sure my index cards were safe, but the only thing in there was a tissue. I stood up in a panic and felt my back pockets: comb, wallet. Then I remembered I had moved the cards to the breast pocket of my

84 · Chapter Ten

jacket during the cocktail hour. I reached into my jacket pocket, pulled them out, and breathed a sigh of relief. As I did, I realized that the entire table was watching me in silence.

"I believe you've answered my question," said Simon. "You couldn't have possibly worked for me."

Everyone at the table, including Michael, laughed as I sat down.

Except Emily. She turned to me and spoke loudly enough for Simon to hear.

"He said you looked familiar, and he wanted to know if you've ever worked at that dreadful little magazine *Gloss*. I can't imagine you would have..."

"Oh," I said, "I'm sorry, Mr. Bell. I've never worked at *Gloss*. Maybe you just know my face from the elevator."

"'Mr. Bell'—very nice. But you can call me Simon. And you are?"

"Paul. Paul Cavanaugh. I work in marketing."

"Paul reports to me," said Michael, annoyingly.

Simon flashed a half smile at Emily, but otherwise ignored her snarky reference to *Gloss*—the magazine where he had made his name by setting a company-wide record of 189 ad pages in a single issue. The record still stood.

"It's a pleasure to meet you, Paul," he said as a waiter handed him his drink. "But I do know your face from somewhere other than the elevators."

"Well, I am good friends with your corporate marketing director. John Steffans."

"That's it! I've seen you out and about with John, haven't I? Thick as thieves, the two of you..."

"I suppose I'm a bad influence on him."

"No matter," said Simon, raising his glass. "Any friend of the finest marketing mind in publishing is a friend of mine."

He took a long sip and then motioned to the waiter.

"Another round for the table, mate..."

I took an equally long sip of my Amstel Light to keep up. I

didn't love Amstel, but I had thought it a good idea to drink what Mitch was drinking. Simon noted the brand.

"...and switch my friend Paul over there to a man's beer. My God, mate, Steffans would be ashamed of you."

Simon spotted an old colleague at another table and motioned him over. Emily tapped me on the knee as the two of them talked.

"Quite the character, isn't he?"

"Yes. My old boss works for him. The stories he's told me..."

"Whatever," said Emily as she touched my forearm again. "I want to hear your story, Paul the Presentation Maker..."

I pressed my hand against the outside of my pants pocket to feel Diane's note.

"...and, by the way," she added, "what did you misplace earlier that had you so startled?"

"Oh, nothing. Just my index cards. I have to give a presentation tomorrow and I've been practicing as often as I can."

"Relax. I'm sure you're ready. You'll do great. I have a feeling about you."

I noted to myself the irony that she had largely paraphrased Diane's note. She touched my forearm once again, with a light stroke this time, and I felt a rush of excitement. I slipped my other hand inside my pocket and clutched Diane's note just as the waiter placed a Heineken in front of me. I pulled away from Emily, picked it up, and took a sip.

"Thanks for the manly beer," I shouted across to Simon, who barely nodded back—as if to convey that bantering with legends was subject to a time limit.

A microphone crackled and a voice filled the room.

"Good evening, all," said Mitch, standing in front of a floor to ceiling window overlooking the bright lights of Midtown.

The room quieted and virtually everyone turned their attention to him. Simon dabbed a piece of bread in a small plate of oil.

"First, I want to thank the entire team for a great first day. I think we all got a lot out of it. I'm really excited about what's ahead for us—not just tomorrow but in the year ahead. I also want to thank Henry Wallace and our editorial guests for an illuminating panel discussion."

He paused as applause filled the room.

"We're also looking forward to hearing from Henry tomorrow on some *Bellwether* special issues planned for next year. In addition, you'll all have a chance to speak directly with Carlyle Nash's senior executive team. That panel is the first thing on tomorrow's agenda, so don't let our special guest Simon Bell keep you out late tonight."

Simon stood up and raised his glass.

"Full bar in my limousine, people. All welcome."

The crowd dutifully roared as he sat back down. He never once looked at Mitch, who smiled self-confidently and clapped along in performance.

"And finally, I want to welcome our new sales rep in *Bellwether*'s Los Angeles office. It's not easy starting a new job at a national sales meeting filled with unfamiliar faces, but I think he's fitting in already. Please welcome Thad Bellows. He's a real pro...and I think you're all going to love him."

Thad stood up and bowed majestically. My first impression was that he was a total asshole.

Michael waved at me from across the table.

"Paul," he said. "Come here for a second, will you?"

I excused myself to Emily, with a mixture of relief and yearning. On the one hand, the instant spark I had felt between us made me want to run to my hotel room, lock the door, and call Diane. On the other, I wanted to take Emily by the hand and run off together into the city night. With her every light touch of my forearm, I had felt increasingly aware of how less and less carefree my life was becoming. As I circled the table, I lamented that both she and Simon—now ordering shots for the table— had knocked me off focus. I just wanted to find a corner and read my index cards. I took a knee next to Michael's chair. He wiped a few beads of sweat from his brow.

"What's up?" I asked.

"Are you ready for your presentation tomorrow?"

"I think so. Yeah…I feel pretty good about. I think the content is—"

"Can you help me with mine?"

I wanted to say "You've got to be fucking kidding me," but all that came out was, "Sure, Michael." He wasn't ready!? And how much help did he need?

"Great, thanks," he said. "I told the audiovisual guys that I would have my last few slides to them by midnight. I have most of it written out, but you know how bad I am in PowerPoint."

"How many is a few?"

I stole a look across the table. Simon had moved to my chair and was talking to Emily. They knocked back shots of Jameson and laughed. Relief ebbed, rage flowed. Rage ebbed, relief flowed. I reached across Michael to Simon's empty place setting and picked up his shot glass.

"What the hell are you doing?" asked Michael.

"Fuck it. He drank mine. How many slides are we talking about?"

"Like twelve or so…maybe fifteen."

"Fifteen? Shit, Michael."

"I know, I'm sorry," he said as he rubbed his temples.

I sighed.

"Alright, I guess we'll go to your room after we eat."

The waiter began serving salads to the table. Simon showed no signs of leaving my chair, so I sat down at his. He shot me a devilish grin and raised his glass. Emily rested her chin atop folded hands and mouthed five words to me. I couldn't make them out, so I leaned forward and tapped my ear. But Simon was already swinging back into her space, so she turned to him in conversation. The first word might have been "Meet," but rather than focus on it, I willfully closed my eyes and wondered what Diane was doing at the moment. I saw her reading a book, under low light, with our black-and-white cat curled up on her lap.

Michael was writing presentation notes on the back of his dinner menu. I flipped mine to the blank side and slid it to him. It looked like he would need the space. I quietly ate my salad and gazed out at the room. The layout reminded me of my wedding reception—just without the separate table for the bridal party and throne-like chairs for the bride and groom. I recalled eating my salad awkwardly with my left hand that night.

I had been holding Diane's hand with my right. ▪

CHAPTER ELEVEN

World Inventory
(2007)

TALL TO BEGIN WITH, Paige was wearing impossibly high heels when she paused outside my office door after the breakfast meeting, dragging a large cardboard box filled with beach balls toward Mitch's office.

"You're helping me with my résumé later," she said.

"I can't. I have to leave early to pick up Aidan."

"Tomorrow then."

"Aren't you happy about the days off?" I asked as I removed my glasses.

She came in and sat down.

"Sure, but they aren't going to change the fact that my job stinks. Look at me, Paul. I'm dragging a box of inflatables around in Chanel, which I suppose is better than how my day started—making sure Mitch's favorite cream cheese was on the table. And he didn't even eat!"

I handed her a bottle of water and chugged mine.

"Thanks," she said. "Why did you change your hair, by the way?"

"You don't like it?"

"No. It looks OK. Just different. You can always go back and forth."

"You know what, Paige? I really don't give a shit about my hair."

"You look tired, Paul."

I was getting tired of people telling me I looked tired. I put my glasses back on.

"Can't sleep," I said as the phone rang.

It was Naomi calling for Mitch. I picked up with a "Hey."

"Is Paige in your office?" asked Naomi.

"Yep."

"Mitch is ready for her and he needs you too."

"Fuck."

"I'll take that to mean you're on your way."

"Be right there," I sighed.

We stood to go.

"Oh, your incentive card," Paige reminded me.

"Right." I pulled the card I'd taken off Mary Ellen's beach ball out of my back pocket and handed it over.

"Thanks."

I took the back end of the box of beach balls and helped Paige carry it down the hall. Peering into the box, I saw that most of the balls still had their cards attached and a handful of loose cards were clipped to the lip of the box with a medium binder clip.

"Did you get them all back?" I asked as we headed for Mitch's office.

"No, I'm short one," Paige said without looking back. "But I'm not going to worry about it. I can't imagine Mitch is going to count them."

Naomi motioned us to go ahead in. Thad was sitting on the couch against the far window, the trees of Bryant Park behind him in the distance. Mitch was doing his daily dance with Lou Lamont.

"Not true, Lou. IBM is locked in. Hal Franks is a big believer in *World.*"

He shook his head as Lou spoke on the other end. Very faintly, I could hear a teasing chuckle coming through the phone.

"Just hold the article, Lou, alright? If you run it based on nothing but a rumor, I'll be the one laughing tomorrow."

He fielded another question as he penned a one-sentence note and affixed it to a copy of *World* with a gold paper clip.

"Christ, Lou. You want to talk about circulation too? Let me buy you lunch today."

At this point, a normal observer would have become mildly concerned that the magazine he worked for was coming under increased scrutiny based on potentially worrisome trends. But as I watched Mitch squirm just a bit, I found myself enjoying it. He had been conducting press coverage of his projects like a maestro for so long that it was perversely thrilling to hear a few missed notes in his symphony.

"OK, next week then." he said. "I'll have Naomi find a day."

And now Lou Lamont was saying no to a steak. I turned to see if Thad and Paige had been listening too, but Thad—with a look of anguish—was polishing a scuffed shoe, and Paige was working headhunters on her Blackberry.

I didn't want Mitch to realize how closely I'd been observing him, so I took my glasses off and rubbed my eyes.

"Since when do you wear glasses, Paul?" asked Mitch.

"I wear them once in a while. Maybe you just didn't notice."

Had he been genuinely interested, he would have said, "That's impossible"—because we both knew Mitch didn't miss anything—but he just shrugged.

"I'm going to email you some talking points later. I need another turnaround paper."

Great, I thought. Diane's coming home tonight and the first thing I'll have to tell her is that I brought work home.

"Can we talk about it now?" I asked.

"Not yet," said Mitch. He got up and walked over to the box of beach balls. Paige set her Blackberry down and tensed up.

"All set," she said.

Mitch picked one up.

"Are they all in there?"

"I'm pretty sure," she said as she shifted in her chair.

"Did you count them?"

"Really Mitch?"

He stiffened and stared at her. Paige's eyes widened in response to what looked like genuine retinal contact from Mitch. I tried to track a line from his eyes to hers to confirm it. Paige seemed to shrink, crossing her arms across her chest and pressing her knees together.

"Paige," he said coldly. "This might seem like a ridiculous task to you, but it's important that my orders be followed to the letter. This promotion was clearly a mistake due to the product recall. We can all accept a share of the blame, but I would hate for this situation to impact the reputation of anyone with oversight of the promotions department of this magazine. Am I understood?"

"Yes Mitch."

"Thank you, Paige. Breakfast was excellent this morning, by the way."

"Thanks Mitch," said Paige as she rose to recount the beach balls.

"Thad had a great idea," Mitch continued. "Since we have a four-day weekend coming, let's have a staff outing tomorrow night. Somewhere fun. Let's boost morale sky-high."

Paige sagged, knowing she would have to organize the event in just 24 hours. I sagged too because I would have to tell Diane I'd be going out to yet another party, on her first full night back. Thad clapped happily, probably thinking about what he would wear.

Paige completed her recount.

"Sixty-nine beach balls, sixty-nine tags. There's one missing."

"Please track it down," said Mitch. "Leave the box here. Naomi will have Office Services get rid of them."

Paige looked to me for sympathy. I shrugged, sat back and thought about the missing card—currently stuck to my fridge—and the beach ball itself. It was still in Aidan's crib, and perfectly safe to lick.

* * * *

I PICKED UP AIDAN AT ABOUT 3:30 and headed straight for the Seaford-Oyster Bay Expressway, a short thorough-fare that traversed our section of Long Island from north to south. I wanted him to take an afternoon nap, and the only way to get him to do that was to drive up and down until he fell asleep. He would fight me if I put him in his crib awake. I multitasked throughout the drive, one hand on the wheel and one lifting a cheeseburger to my mouth. Between bites, I set the burger down on the front seat beside me. There was no center console in the old Malibu, just a long front seat. When Diane and I were dating, she used to snuggle beside me as I drove her home.

My Blackberry was on the seat too. I picked it up and saw that Mitch had emailed about the next turnaround paper. Aidan wailed for another French fry, so I reached back and put three into his chubby little hand. He smiled wide and gnawed away.

"They'll be cracking open our chests by fifty, little man."

I poured the rest of the fries out on the burger wrapper next to me and flashed him the empty container.

"No more. See, boy? Go to sleep. Sleepy sleepy."

He wailed some more. I threw another fry back and it landed between his leg and the edge of his car seat. He plunged his hand down and hunted for it.

I returned my eyes to the road and saw that I was at the south-ern end of the expressway, so I exited and looped back north. I gunned the eight-cylinder engine hard as I merged, then settled into the right lane to read Mitch's email.

The good news was that the paper would largely have to hit on the same themes as the one I'd done that had turned around

Providence Insurance. It would be a quick repurpose that I would be able to finish before Diane came home. The bad news: it was for Hal Franks at IBM.

World was in a tailspin. Why was I laughing?

* * * *

DIANE WAS EAGER TO SEE AIDAN, but her flight was delayed, so I had to put him to bed before she came home. I was more nervous than excited to see her. The fight we had had before she left had been different than any before it. Anger and resentment had been building since the day I joined *World*, but, until that fight, heated discussions about the toll the magazine was taking on us had always found their way to a temporary détente. Not that time. A sense that she was throwing in the towel had hung over every call and email since she'd left.

The flight delay was convenient for me because the IBM turnaround paper took longer than I expected. Mitch kept peppering me with new thoughts via email and I dutifully worked them into the text. His last email of the night—*OK. Got it from here*—arrived just as the airport car service pulled into the driveway. The windows were open in the kitchen, so I could hear Diane using her cheerful voice to thank the driver.

I realized I was holding my Blackberry, so I set it to vibrate and put it in my pocket. I checked my look in the mirror—hair back to normal after a much-needed shower—and noted that I really did look tired. I heard the wheels of Diane's suitcase bump along the paving stones of the front walkway, so I headed to the door to help her in.

She looked tan, rested, but wistful…or sad.

"Hi honey," I said.

I hugged her and kissed her cheek, but she kept one hand on the suitcase. The other held her house keys. I guess she hadn't been sure that I'd even be home to open the door. But I was, and I felt like I deserved credit for it.

"Hi," she said.

"That's it?"

She looked at me in silent amazement for a few seconds.

"Yes, Paul. For now at least."

She entered ahead of me and looked around. I had straightened up pretty well. As she headed for the bathroom and shut the door, my Blackberry vibrated. I set my mind to ignore it and filled a tea kettle instead. I put two cups out on the table and sat down, wondering if it was Mitch emailing. Diane hadn't flushed yet, so I figured I would peek at the subject line.

It was blank. The sender: Thad. A feeling of dread accompanied just about any email from him, because he always had an ulterior, political motive—especially if he cc'd Mitch. I drummed my fingers on the table and told myself to just leave the email for the morning and focus on Diane. The tea kettle began its low-boil hum. Diane was still in the bathroom. I opened the email. Mitch was cc'd.

Paul: STILL waiting on that World vs. Globalist presentation. Next week's sales meeting? —TB

Classic fucking Thad. He knew exactly what he was doing. While everyone was looking forward to a four-day weekend, he was intent on ruining mine. But that was only if Mitch cared about the presentation too. Thad had been bringing up the topic for weeks, but never once had Mitch indicated that he agreed on the need for it. Until he did, I would keep deprioritizing it. As I mulled over a good response, Mitch chimed in:

Yes, let's get that done, Paul.

I pounded the kitchen table lightly. Diane flushed and turned on the faucet. As I put the Blackberry away, the kettle started whistling. Diane rushed out of the bathroom as I rose to take it off the burner.

"For God's sake, Paul, are you trying to wake Aidan up?"

"I'm sorry, I'm sorry. I was...cleaning a dish."

She walked over slowly and started frisking me.

"Unbelievable," she said. "Where is it?"

I handed the Blackberry over. Diane sat down at the kitchen island and put her head in her hands.

"Diane, I swear to God, I wasn't even looking at it, but then Thad emailed. I only checked because I thought it was nothing, but it has to do with a project. All I need to do is confirm, so if you could please give the Blackberry back after we're done catching up…"

"Don't tell me. Mitch is cc'd."

"Yes. All I have to respond with is 'Will do.'"

"I'll do it," she said as she scrolled to the email.

I hurried to her side.

"Oh come on, Diane. I'll do it."

But she turned her back, tapped the email out and sent it.

"Done," she said. "I wrote 'I quit.'"

"Are you serious!?" I said as I made a grab for the device.

"No, you idiot," she replied, showing me the sent email: "Will do."

I breathed a sigh of relief.

"Can we have the tea now?" said Diane. "Before I punch you?"

I poured her a cup.

"I'm sorry about what happened before your trip."

"I know you're sorry, Paul. But it doesn't mean anything if things don't change. Please don't tell me about how important *World* is. I know it's 'important' relative to the media world, but it's just a job in the end. You've got to learn how to leave it there at least once in a while. Even if I agreed that it's the most important thing anyone has ever worked on, that's still no excuse for it being more important to you than your wife and child."

"That's not fair, Diane. That's not true. How can you say that?"

"Please, Paul, I don't want to go through all this again. I'll just get angry. And I don't want to cry."

As she spoke, I was doing a quick calculus in my head. The only way I would be able to make serious headway on the presentation would be if I went in to the office on one of the two off days. Thursday was out because I'd probably be partying late Wednesday night. It would have to be Friday.

"I understand," I said. "I'm sorry. I don't want to get angry either. But listen, I have good news. Mitch gave us all off on Thursday."

"Really? Why?"

"It's an appreciation thing. We've been working our asses off, and things have been a little challenging on the PR front. He wants to boost morale. There are also drinks after work tomorrow night…"

I braced myself.

"Of course there are," she sighed.

"But wait until you hear what's really going on."

I began telling her about the beach ball machinations, leaving out a few details that might worry her. I sensed that she wasn't paying all that much attention when she crossed to the counter and began sorting through mail.

"Are you listening?" I asked.

"I'm listening. It just sounds like you're overthinking the whole thing. It's a beach ball, Paul. Have you lost your mind?"

"You don't understand Mitch like I do, Diane."

"Fine, Paul. Listen…I just don't want to talk about Mitch or *World* or whatever. You should go to bed. You look tired."

"I'm fine. Just working hard."

"Well, I'm tired. It was a horrendous flight…"

She turned and stared sternly.

"…and because someone didn't take Aidan to his pediatrician appointment, I have to take him first thing tomorrow, thank you."

I looked at the floor.

"I got stuck at work. A Honda fire drill. I just couldn't—"

"Yes, Paul," she said, turning her back to me. "I know. You couldn't leave."

She reached for the phone and dialed.

"I have to call your mother before it gets too late. You should go to bed."

"OK," I said. "Can I—"

She slid the Blackberry across the island as my mother picked up. ▪

CHAPTER TWELVE

Paul of *Bellwether*
(2005)

B Y THE TIME I left Michael's hotel room, his presentation on *Bellwether*'s 18-month marketing plan was in solid shape. I wasn't sure how well he would deliver it the next day, however, because his nerves seemed to be getting the best of him.

"Wait, wait," he said as I started for the door. "Why am I clicking twice on slide eleven?"

I sighed.

"Because it's a build, Michael. If the second bar of the chart is up on the screen before you've explained the context, it completely negates the impact. Think about it for a second. Without the build, it's like starting a joke with the punch line."

He clicked back and forth with his brow furrowed. *This is my boss*, I thought, *and he went to Northwestern*. I had worked with about 30 guys behind deli counters and in bars who could have grasped the concept more quickly.

"Oh, OK," he said finally. "I see what you mean."

I could tell he didn't, but I needed to get to my room to take a last run through my own presentation and to get some sleep.

"You're ready. You'll be great," I said.

As I walked down the hallway, I briefly wondered if anything had happened between Simon and Emily. Neither would be in attendance the next day, so I imagined them cruising down the West Side Highway that very moment in Simon's limo—him with a champagne glass in hand, her naked and mounting him. I, meanwhile, would have to content myself with a beer from the minibar and my index cards.

I ran through my presentation a few more times and finally told myself that I was as ready as I'd ever be. I called Diane and we talked about our days. As she went on about a fellow social worker named Florence, or Flora, I pondered whether to tell her about the interesting people I had been seated with at dinner. I did, but I left out Emily Frazier.

* * * *

MICHAEL'S PRESENTATION opened Day Two right after breakfast. He did fine—benefitting somewhat from the relative inattention of the hungover crowd, as well as from the fact that the marketing plan was based largely on Mitch's overall strategy. He closed to light, obligatory applause.

By mid-morning, the audience had perked up and was all ears for the 10:30 address from Henry Wallace. A longtime writer for the magazine, he had been elevated to editor following the exit of Cassandra White—an often-controversial British media maven who had succeeded in shaking off *Bellwether*'s stuffy image. In his first year, Henry was doing a stellar job of maintaining the magazine's buzz while lowering the drama. I was most interested in hearing what he had to say about the sports issue, as I didn't want my presentation to seem at all redundant.

I was seated on the aisle in the 20th row of the auditorium. I would be presenting at 11:30 and my body pulsated with nervous energy. I breathed deeply and focused on Henry as he worked his way to the sports issue. He gave a quick rundown of prospective writers and subjects while, thankfully, mentioning nothing about the history of sports coverage in the magazine. I made a few notes as he summed up.

"You know," he said, "when I was a writer under Cassandra, I once told her we should do an issue on sports. But she just looked at me and said "Ohhhh, running, jumping...who gives a fuck."

The audience laughed hard and I did too. A short time later, Henry exited to loud applause and we broke for 15-minutes. Michael sidled up to me as we headed toward the auditorium exit.

"Thanks again for all your help," he said.

"My pleasure, boss. Nice job."

"You think? Mitch read emails the whole time."

"Yeah. But I think he's been doing that through every presentation...except Henry's. He'll probably go take a dump during mine."

"You ready?"

"I think so."

A table of snacks and beverages sat just outside the auditorium's doors and was being mobbed by my colleagues, all complaining that this was the only break of the day except for lunch. Mitch had jammed in two more afternoon sessions overnight. There was a line for the men's room, so I hustled upstairs to my hotel room.

Nerves were causing me to sweat. I rinsed my face and looked in the mirror. The dress code for the day was casual, so I was wearing a blue button-down dress shirt. Sweat circles were seeping visibly from the underarms.

"Shit."

It was the only shirt I had packed for the day so I took it off and began blowing the wet spots with a hair dryer. I was simultaneously reciting the opening of my presentation when the words came to me, out of the ether.

Running, jumping, I...

I propped the hair dryer up on the sink and draped the second sweat circle over it. I hurried to the night stand to grab a blank index card and the words of a new opening poured out. I noted that with just eight minutes to go before my presentation, it was an awfully inconvenient time to have a creative burst. But I knew it was a good one. I breathed deeply to calm myself, read it a few times in succession, then recited it from memory a few more.

Would Uncle Frank change his opening at the last minute? Yeah, I think he would. Dad would probably call us both crazy.

The hair dryer shorted out just as my shirt began giving off a scent of burning cotton with a hint of Right Guard. I picked it up and saw that I had done an adequate job on one side, but had branded the other with a dark brown circle. At least it hadn't burned through. I put the shirt back on and made a note not to raise my arms.

I recited my opening again as I exited my room, only to be stopped two strides down the hallway by a bellhop.

"Mr. Cavanaugh?"

"Yes."

He handed me a note.

This was left for you at the front desk by a woman who checked out this morning.

"Thank you," I said as I grabbed the note and raced to the elevator. In the envelope, written on hotel stationery:

"Peter— It was lovely meeting you last night. So sorry our conversation was cut short. I had no choice but to retire early and alone, lamenting my weakness for men of Irish descent. I do hope we can connect again when I'm back in the States. Warm regards, Emily. P.S. Good luck presenting. Freckles forward.

My head spun as the elevator stopped a floor away from the auditorium. A group of four tourists crowded on with their bags. I looked at my watch and saw that I was a minute past break time.

I was stunned and flattered to think that Emily had been lying in bed thinking about me. The image gave me an erection. Then I visualized Diane walking in on us. I recited my opening again. The doors opened and I dashed out ahead of the tourists.

The meeting had begun as I downshifted through the doors. Michael was at the podium.

"...So to help you sell the heck out of these special issues, the marketing team has created custom sales tools for each one. First up is Paul Cavanaugh to take you through the sports issue presentation. Paul..."

The room was quiet as I strode down the aisle and then climbed the side steps to the stage. The cover slide of my presentation was projected on a large screen stage left, the podium was stage right, and Mitch was seated dead center in the first row.

I reached into my left pants pocket, pulled out my index cards, and placed them on the right side of the podium. Emily's note was on top. I paused for a moment and put it in my left pants pocket. I casually slipped my right hand into my right pocket and felt for Diane's note.

Start...now, said Uncle Frank.

I slipped my left hand back into my left pocket and felt Emily's note too. *Unbelievable. I could have had sex with another woman last night.*

I looked out at the audience. I smiled. I felt calm.

"Good morning. You know...I was very happy to be asked to do the sports presentation. Because I am a big fan. I don't paint my face or hurl batteries from the upper deck, but let's just say... 'Running, jumping'..."

I paused a beat and leaned on the podium, earnestly.

"...I give a fuck."

The audience roared.

Listen. Wait, said Uncle Frank.

I backed up a step, smiled modestly, and let the sound wash over me. It was like a drug.

I looked down at Mitch. He wasn't reading emails.

He sat back smiling and chuckling. He slowly and coolly clapped. A laughing Dan Hadley from our Midwest office, seated next to him, said something and Mitch nodded and laughed some more.

I smiled and continued with the meat of the presentation. I felt relaxed and in charge—so different than I did in one-on-one office discussions in which I was typically less forceful and confident in my ideas. I even left the podium a few times to wander the stage and illustrate points on the screen. The real passion I had developed for *Bellwether* came through.

At the end of the presentation, I handled a pair of questions with ease. There was just one more. It came from our new sales rep from the West Coast: Thad Bellows.

"Hi. I think there's a lot of great stuff in there, but isn't it a little heavy on editorial retrospective? My clients might want to hear a bit more about the readership and its interest in sports."

Who is this fucking asshole again?

Michael stood up.

"I think I can answer that," he said. "We'll be happy to provide some readership stats separately, but Paul was specifically asked to take this tack with the deck. Many of our clients might scratch their heads at the thought of a *Bellwether* sports issue. We're looking to address their reservations head-on, and I think Paul has hit it out of the park."

The audience clapped in agreement. I felt guilty for ever bitching about Michael to Diane. He was a stand-up guy.

"That's it, I guess." I said. "Thanks, everyone."

More applause. I couldn't wait to call Diane.

And I wondered what I would email to Emily.

* * * *

THE CLOSING DINNER WAS A CASUAL AFFAIR, and if people had drunk more than they thought they would on the previous night, they were drinking double that now. Wine flowed, shots were downed, special-themed tequila cocktails came around on trays that were quickly emptied. An impromptu dance floor was set up in the middle of the hotel restaurant and the staff packed sweatily in.

I stayed on the outskirts with Michael, Dan Hadley, and a couple of guys from the art department. I downed two tequilas before switching to an Amstel as I noticed Mitch entering late.

Dan was talking bullishly about Midwest sales prospects, but I was hardly listening. I watched Mitch across the room as one pretty female staffer after another engaged him in brief conversation. As he drifted from person to person, an Amstel in hand, I observed that he barely ever spoke to anyone for more than a minute or two—men and beautiful women alike. I supposed that most people would chalk this up to his being a reserved man and devoted husband, but I began to think it was something else: a fiercely consistent habit of guarding his reputation. I had learned pretty quickly that in the world of Carlyle Nash, publishers and senior corporate executives could have virtually anything and anyone they wanted. Most took all of it. Even the ones who took just a little were subject to gossip and the wildest of rumors. But not Mitch. There was one thing people could say about him and one thing only: he turned dying magazines around. As I watched him float through the party, I realized that he was intent on making sure that it would be the only thing he was known for. He worked his way to our group. I turned my Amstel label to the front.

"Hello gentlemen," he said.

"Hey Mitch," said Michael.

"Try the tequila, Mitch," said Dan.

"Thanks Dan. But I'm good with this."

"Great Day Two," said Michael.

"Yes," Mitch replied. "Really productive. Good stuff."

He was already pulling away, about to move on to the next group, the next surface chat. I resigned myself to the fact that no praise for my presentation would be forthcoming. I reached for a mini empanada on a passing tray. Mitch looked at me as

I put it in my mouth. He extended his Amstel and clinked it against mine.

"Well done today...Paul." ▪

CHAPTER THIRTEEN

The *World* Runs on Steak

(2007)

I HAD YET TO EVEN LOG ON to my computer on Wednesday when Mitch called and asked me to come by his office. I was wearing a clean suit for the first time since Friday, so I left the jacket on. For the sake of continuity, I was once again wearing my hair slicked back. Diane, who had slept in the glider next to Aidan's crib, had looked up at me like I was a stranger when I'd said goodbye that morning.

"Who, what?" she had sleepily asked.

"George Clooney. Have a great day."

Mitch had taken a call when I got to his office, so he motioned me to remain outside. With Naomi not in yet, I sat down at her desk. There was a copy of *Media Times* in her inbox so I picked it up and began leafing through it. Toward the back, there was a photo page recapping industry soirées of the past week or two. Each shot was of the standard variety: four or five smiling executives shoulder to shoulder at an awards banquet; an editorial team posing with a celebrity cover subject at a sponsored event. In the lower right, there was a picture of Mitch at the *Media Times* Innovators Summit. Three industry notables stood to his right, and I saw a familiar face to his left. I checked the caption to make sure it was who I thought it was. Yes. It was my old *Bellwether* boss, Michael Pace. Michael's long-rumored departure for Jessup & Greer had happened shortly before Mitch moved to *World*, clearing my path to the Marketing Director spot at *World*. His exit had been convenient to say the least. But now here he was hobnobbing with his old pal Mitch at an industry event. My left eyelid began to twitch.

What the hell is going on? Did they just bump into each other? Or did they plan to meet up? There was a lot of turmoil at Jessup & Greer these days. A couple of the magazines weren't doing so well, and rumor had it that Mack Howell would be out as CEO as soon as they found his successor, someone who could shake things up. Maybe Michael was feeling insecure. *Is Mitch recruiting Michael back to Carlyle Nash? Is he planning on bringing him in at* World? *Over me!? Did I botch the IBM turnaround? Is that fucking cocksucker Thad turning Mitch against me? Is it my hair? Or, fuck…did he figure out that I have the beach ball? Did he check the security video and see me walking away from Mary Ellen's cubicle? No, wait, even if he did, he wouldn't know I had the beach ball. I deflated it and stuck it down the back of my pants. No, no, no—it can't be that. I'm just not getting the job done anymore. That must be it. He's bringing Michael back. I fucking know it.*

I pulled my wallet out of my pants pocket and checked to make sure I still had the incentive card. Yes. I'd taken to carrying it with me everywhere lately. I put my wallet back in my pocket and tried to eavesdrop on Mitch's phone call by rolling Naomi's chair a bit closer to his door. He was practically whispering on the phone.

I don't believe it. I think he's talking to Michael.

I rolled a bit closer.

"OK, bye," he said. "Love you too."

I rolled back to Naomi's desk.

"Paul," Mitch shouted, "Come on in."

I entered and sat down without saying a word. The box of beach balls had been moved behind his desk and taped shut. Mitch's fencing foil lay on top of it, as if protecting them. He was crossing an item off his to-do list—"Call wife...express love," I presumed. He looked up in mild surprise that I hadn't entered with my usual "What can I do for you, Mitch?"

"Sticking with the slick look, I see."

"Easier to manage," I replied.

"It looks good. You should keep it."

It was the first time Mitch had ever complimented me on something not related to work. Or maybe it *was* related to work in some way. Perhaps he was signaling that it was time for me to focus more on image than substance. Maybe he wanted me to start rubbing elbows at industry summits like Michael.

"Thanks," I said. "I just saw your picture in *Media Times*. The Innovators Summit..."

"Real snooze," said Mitch as he sharpened a pencil. "Ran into Michael Pace there. He sends his best."

I felt a sense of relief that he wasn't hiding their meeting. Perhaps I was just being paranoid.

"Oh, wow. I haven't seen Michael in—"

"Yeah, so listen," he said, "I need a favor. As you may have noticed, Lou Lamont is becoming a bit harder to manage these days..."

I sat up in my chair, flattered that he was enlisting my help in manipulating the press, while thrilling to the notion that he was about to show me his hand. I nearly chuckled at the thought that I was serving as both friend and foe. I covered with a cough.

"...so I want to send him something. Naomi is out, so can you stop at Del Frisco's today and get him a gift card? He loves steaks."

"Sure Mitch. No problem."

"Two hundred dollars. Just expense it. Then messenger it to him with this."

He wrote out a quick note, sealed it in an envelope, and pushed it across the desk.

"I'll take care of it," I said, standing up.

"Thanks Paul. Keep it between us."

"Of course, Mitch."

* * * *

I PLANNED ON HEADING OUT to Del Frisco's right before noon, but Lily and Matt walked in to catch me up on a few projects for sales reps as I was about to leave.

I dutifully listened and added my two cents here and there, but mostly nodded along and said "Good" or "Great" or "Nice work" where applicable.

Lily, seeming tired and a bit impatient, rose to leave first.

"See you around," she said sarcastically.

"If you're lucky," I shot back.

Matt, a recent business school grad Lily and I had hired as an associate six months earlier, lingered.

"Hey, Paul. Can I talk to you?"

"Sure. But I have to run in a couple of minutes. What's up?"

He shifted in his chair.

"Well…I'm just wondering how I'm doing. You OK with me? My work?"

For God's sake, I thought. *I don't need this shit right now.*

"What are you talking about? You're doing fantastic work here, Mark. No news is good news with me."

I started putting on my jacket.

"My name is Matt, Paul."

"Huh? Matt, yeah, I know. What did I call you?"

"You called me Mark."

"Shit, sorry," I said. "I have nephews named Mark and Matt, and I get them mixed up all the time."

Their names were actually Adam and Alex, but close enough.

"It's OK," he said. "I know you're under a lot of stress right now and—"

"Uh, no Matt, I'm solid right now. Things are good here. Listen, it sounds like you have a couple of things on your plate, so why don't we grab breakfast on Friday?"

"We're closed Friday, Paul."

"Oh yeah, right. Well, we'll get something on the calendar next week. But don't worry, man. You're golden with me. And Mitch knows too."

"Really? Mitch has mentioned me?"

"Yeah," I said as we headed for the door. "You're solid all around. I'll see you when I get back."

Del Frisco's was just a handful of blocks away, but I jumped in a cab anyway. The driver looked at me like I was the laziest man on the planet, but I didn't feel like sweating—and I planned on expensing the shit out of running errands for Mitch. As we turned onto Sixth Avenue, traffic was at a virtual standstill. I watched the meter slowly climb to $4.00 and then handed the driver a five.

"This was stupid," I said.

"Yes, it was," he said, handing me the receipt.

I walked the rest of the way and headed straight to the bar on arrival. I grabbed a stack of cocktail napkins and patted my face and neck.

The bartender came over and barely nodded.

"Absolut cranberry and a menu, please."

The restaurant slowly began to fill as I tried to decide between a grilled chicken Caesar salad and steak tips. I went with the salad. My drink was down to the ice when I felt a stinging middle-finger flick on the back of my neck. I spun around.

"What the fuck—"

It was John.

"Hey, asshole," he said.

"Motherfucker. That hurt."

He sat down next to me and motioned to the bartender.

"That's what you get for screening my calls all morning," he said. "But I get it. You'd rather eat lunch alone like some sad sack than hang out with me."

"That's not it..."

"I know, I know. I'm just fucking with you, Paul. What are you drinking?"

"Vodka cranberry."

"Two more of these," John said to the passing mute bartender.

"What are you doing here?" I asked.

"Meeting Simon. He wants to have a working lunch. I have to write him a eulogy for Bill Burns. Massive heart attack at his desk. He worked for Simon for twenty years, but Simon can't string together a few nice thoughts on his own."

"That's why they pay you the big bucks."

"Yeah, whatever," said John as he chewed on a swizzle stick. "It's better than working on another presentation. Shit's destroying my soul. What's up with you? They kill your flop of a magazine yet?"

"Come on. Way early for that to happen."

"I don't know, I don't know," he teased. "Economy's starting to wheeze a little. I'm just glad I'm not working for the McMansion of magazines like you."

I laughed.

"Maybe I'll finally have to come work for you."

"Yeah right. You'll just say no again. That door is just about closed, you cock tease."

As I stirred my drink, I considered telling John about the beach ball situation. I felt frustrated that Diane didn't grasp its significance. I needed someone to see it the way I did, and I thought John would be the right sounding board. I'd always felt that, underneath the cynicism and world-weariness, he was a man with a moral code and a friend I could trust.

"I have to show you something," I said, reaching for my wallet and pulling out the incentive card.

"Read this. But keep it between us, please."

"Of course," he said, and gave it a quick glance.

"There's no fucking way you guys hit that number."

"Exactly. Do you have a few minutes? When is Simon getting here?"

"We're good. I came early to get drunk."

As he took off his jacket, I launched into the story behind the beach ball, covering every detail, including how I had essentially stolen the missing one, though I didn't say from where. To my delight, John was on the edge of his seat, smiling throughout and asking all the right questions.

"This is great," he laughed. "That thing is your severance, man. Or leverage for a raise. Trust me, if I know Mitch like I think I do, he'll pay to keep that out of the press."

"I guess so. But it's really not about the money."

John looked at me quizzically. "What's it about then?" he asked.

As I took a sip of my drink, I realized I didn't have a very clear answer. John guzzled his drink and looked past me.

"All good things must come to an end," he said. "Simon's here."

I turned toward the entrance of the restaurant. Simon was kissing the hand of the hostess. She appeared to make a comment about his beard. He stroked it and said thank you. He was wearing a grey suit, white shirt, and a pink tie. I could sell any one of the three and have enough for an in-ground pool.

John stood up, reached into his wallet, and threw a pair of $20s on the bar. I expected Simon to head directly to a table and summon John, but he saw us and came over.

"Getting a head start, I see," he said.

"Just one," said John.

"Relax, mate. I'm thirsty myself. And we are mourning a man after all."

Simon looked at me and nodded.

"Afternoon, mate."

"Simon," said John, "this is Paul Cavanaugh. I've been trying to get him to come work with us for years."

"We've met before though, haven't we?" Simon asked.

I extended my hand and he gripped it like a tanker captain. I tried not to wince.

"We have," I said. "At a *Bellwether* sales meeting a few years back."

"That's where Paul and I worked together for a time," said John.

"Yes," said Simon. "I do remember. Are you still there, Paul?"

"No, I moved on to the *World* launch."

"Ahhh, a Mitch Blake acolyte. I'm surprised you still have your hair, mate."

I laughed as the hostess hung back, waiting to escort them to a table. The bartender set down my Caesar salad.

"Is that what you ordered?" asked Simon.

"I hear it's pretty good here," I said.

He looked at John, then back at me.

"A salad...at Del Frisco's. Don't tell me. You bought a new dress you're trying to squeeze into."

He laughed and clapped John on the back. John smiled and shook his head like he'd seen this sort of hazing from Simon for decades.

"I may get a steak too," I said.

Simon took out a $100 bill and dropped it atop John's $20s. He unfolded my dinner napkin and laid it across the salad like a coroner. He turned to the hostess.

"We'll be three, darling." ▪

CHAPTER FOURTEEN

Paint *Bellwether* Black
(2005-06)

"**I**'M TELLING YOU, Paul," said John. "You don't want to do this."

"It's just an email," I said, hovering over my keyboard. "I'm sure nothing will come of it. She lives in London."

John closed the door to my cramped *Bellwether* office.

"Doesn't matter. I've seen her on the elevator at least five times in the past year. I'm sure she has a place here. You'll have plenty of opportunity to fuck her...and fuck up your life."

"At the very least, I have to respond to her note. Common courtesy."

"Do what you want..." he said as he tried to make room for himself at the round table that took up most of my office.

"...but I've been there," he continued. "It's bad news. Just jerk off to her. Anyway, that's not why I stopped by. Kyle just told me he's leaving corporate. I need a new number two. So let me take you out of this shitty little office and get you a window."

I saved a draft of my email and swiveled around.

"Did you know I finally met Simon at our national sales meeting? He was on a panel, and Mitch even invited him to one of the dinners."

"File that under 'Keep your friends close and your enemies closer.' What happened? Did you introduce yourself?"

"No, we were at the same table and one thing led to another. He called you 'the finest marketing mind in publishing.'"

"Yeah, whatever, he always says that. Standard bullshit..."

John caught himself, realizing that he needed to sell me on Simon as much as on the job.

"...Not that I don't appreciate it. He's a good guy. Tolerates my bullshit too. As I've said before, you'd like working for him."

"So why do you only say good things about him when you're trying to get me to come work for you again?"

John and I had had this conversation a few times before, but I had always been focused on *Bellwether*'s profitability goal and proving myself to Mitch. I felt I had gone a long way on the latter with my presentation at the sales meeting, and we were *this close* on the former. To me, once again, the timing for a move wasn't ideal.

"Everyone bitches about their boss," said John. "You answer this question: what did you think of Simon? I bet you liked him."

"I guess I did...but he was trying to fuck Emily."

"A girl strokes your arm a couple of times and now you're jealous? Simon tries to bed every woman he meets."

"It was just the way he went about it."

A sales rep knocked on the door for our scheduled meeting. John held it shut as he stood up to leave.

"Asshole—this is the right move at the right time for your career. So stop being a Mitch Blake fanboy and give this some serious thought. Talk to your wife about it. Preferably before you fuck a woman who's not as pretty as she is."

"You know, calling me an asshole is a funny way to recruit me."

* * * *

I MANAGED TO STRING JOHN ALONG for a few weeks, usually by cancelling lunches at the last second because "a project just came up." More often than not, I wasn't lying. Michael had begun bringing me into meetings with Mitch, and I was reveling in the increased exposure. My only frustration was that I was still doing nearly all the work and Michael was presenting it to Mitch as a team effort. He had, however, gotten me another raise—which I appreciated. But I also knew it couldn't have happened without approval from above. So it seemed pretty clear to me that Mitch knew I was the guy making things happen in marketing.

Diane was happy about the raise, but often too debilitated by morning sickness to talk about my mission to become Mitch's most indispensable player. Nevertheless, she did show interest the day I told her I had seen Michael walk into a Starbucks that morning with Jeanette Holland, a top executive recruiter with deep connections at Jessup & Greer.

"Wow," she said, as she sipped a ginger ale to combat nausea. "Do you think he's leaving?"

"I can only hope," I replied with excitement. "I can't imagine I won't move up if he does. And if not, then maybe I'll accept John's offer."

"John's offer? What are you talking about?"

"Didn't I tell you? A few weeks ago he asked me again if I was interested in a corporate gig."

"No, Paul," Diane said loudly, putting down her ginger ale. "You didn't tell me that. How could you not tell me?"

I thought about all the suggestive emails I'd been preoccupied exchanging with Emily.

"I was busy, Diane. What's the big deal? So I'm telling you now."

She sighed.

"I should know these things, Paul. We make decisions together or not at all, remember? What's the job John's offering?"

"His second-in-command, basically. I would be helping him with whatever big stuff he's working on for Simon and the company in general."

"Maybe it makes sense this time. You love John, you certainly respect his work more than you do Michael's, and to be perfectly honest, I think the whole Mitch obsession thing will only get worse if you move into Michael's job."

I crossed to the refrigerator, took out a beer, and opened it.

"I'm not obsessed with Mitch, Diane," I said, taking a sip. "I just—"

Diane laughed.

"You've got to be kidding me, Paul. For the past three years, it's been nothing but 'Mitch, Mitch, Mitch' around here. Are you delusional?"

I knew she was right, but I held firm.

"It's what I want, Diane. I just don't think my work is done yet at *Bellwether*."

"You don't think your work is done for *Mitch*. And I don't think I'll ever understand that. Please at least consider the corporate job. For me."

"I will, I will, Diane. Just let me see what happens with Michael first. OK?"

"Fine, Paul," she said as she rubbed her belly, "but I hope you mean it."

"I do. I swear."

She stood up and headed to the bathroom as I peeled the label off my beer bottle.

* * * *

I KNEW SOMETHING WAS UP when Michael failed to respond to three consecutive group emails on which Mitch had been cc'd. Normally, when a sales rep sought our help with a big account, Michael would immediately respond with a *We are on this* assurance before calling me or a colleague to do the heavy lifting. But now...silence.

The weekly sales meeting was about to begin. I drummed my fingers on my desk table in anticipation of the announcement I suspected was coming. Word had spread that Mitch had big news for all of us. I slipped my jacket on and headed down the hallway.

Bellwether's main conference room was dominated by an expansive black table. Seated around it were the sales force and the management team. Michael was just off the head, to Mitch's right. The room was rimmed by a long cushioned couch for the support staff. I grabbed a spot between Maria from PR and Chelsea, a sales assistant.

"Hey Thumper," said Chelsea, "what's up with that?"

She gestured to my right knee. I looked down and saw that I was bouncing it up and down rapidly.

"Five cups of coffee," I said. "Gotta cut back."

"You think?" she said with a smile.

As Mitch called the meeting to order, I noticed some activity outside the glass conference room doors: promotion staffers scurrying around in apparent preparation for an event.

"Good morning all," said Mitch. "You'll all be happy to know that we have no agenda today."

He paused and everyone cheered, loudly and long.

"Wow, I must have really been working your asses off."

Laughter filled the room. I watched Michael to see how he was reacting. He was laughing too but looked somewhat like the cat that swallowed the canary. Mitch continued.

"Well, I'm here to tell you that tomorrow's biggest headline in the business section will be...the return to profitability of *Bellwether*."

As the room erupted in cheers, promotion staffers came through the doors with carts of mimosas and finger food. They threw confetti in the air. Balloons were quickly inflated and smacked back and forth around the room. For the next thirty minutes, we celebrated as Mitch circled the room shaking hands and slapping backs. I was in a scrum with a few graphic artists when he passed, but I reached through and shook his hand. He shouted a "Thanks for your hard work" and worked his way back to the front of the room. He called for everyone's attention.

"Wow, what a ride this has been. And there's not a single person in this room whose contributions I don't know about and appreciate. I am forever grateful for the work you've done and the sacrifices you've made. There's only one person I have to single out and it's with some sadness I do so."

As he turned to a sitting Michael, my jaw tightened. Michael stood up.

"Michael Pace," he continued, "who has been an invaluable partner to me and a critical team player, is moving on to Jessup and Greer to be their VP of corporate marketing."

As the standard "Awwwws" greeted the announcement, I tried not to pump my fist. My path to a spot on Mitch's management team had just been cleared. Mitch continued with his praise for Michael, who said a few words in appreciation, but I was already thinking about how to approach Mitch about the promotion. *Should I email him? Call him? Walk right up after the meeting? Ask his assistant for time on his calendar? Talk to Michael first? See if he and Mitch have already talked about me as Michael's natural replacement?*

"Finally," Mitch said, "I have another announcement. I think you all know how important *Bellwether* is to me, but what's even more important to me is this great company. Carlyle Nash is not only the industry's standard-bearer for exceptional content, it's an innovator and a risk-taker. That's why it has decided to take on the most storied magazine category in the industry—global news."

I took a nervous sip of my mimosa. *What's he leading up to?*

"Beginning next month," Mitch continued, "Carlyle Nash will begin laying the groundwork for a new monthly magazine that promises to shake up the category and capture the imagination of the industry…"

No fucking way. He's going to—

"…and I will be leaving *Bellwether* to be the launch publisher of *World* Magazine." ▪

CHAPTER FIFTEEN

World's Biggest Fraud
(2007)

I ATTEMPTED TO EXCUSE MYSELF as Simon ordered a third bottle of wine. I had been "holding it in" for at least 30 minutes—as Simon held forth on digital media growth, Fed policy, Australian Rules Football, sweet potatoes, and who was in the closet at Carlyle Nash.

"The two-thousand-two Hartwell Vineyards, please." he said, "and would you also—"

I accidentally leaned on the prongs of my dessert fork and it flipped upward, clanking loudly off my water glass.

"Forgive my nephew," he said, "I let him have his first drink that wasn't a canned beer."

"Sorry gentlemen," I said.

Simon chuckled.

"No worries, mate."

"Straight back," said John, pointing to the men's room.

I headed toward it at a slow post-Porterhouse pace. My senses were clouded by cabernet and all I could think was that cheese-cake was on the way. Once inside, I splashed cold water on my face and looked at my glassy-eyed reflection. I remembered with dread that the *World* appreciation party was that evening. Clearly, I would need to stop drinking and sleep in my office for a few hours. Just one more glass.

When I returned to my seat, Simon had finally moved on to the reason he'd asked John to lunch in the first place. John produced a legal pad from his bag and set it on the table. He began reading aloud the eulogy draft. Simon stopped him after two paragraphs.

"That's not something I would say. Change it to 'Clearly, I know a thing or two about great men.' Then write 'Pause for laughter' in parentheses."

John tapped his pencil.

"You really think so, Simon? I don't know if that hits the right note. He collapsed at age forty-nine...in the cafeteria...on Take Your Kid to Work Day. It was a bit of a shock."

Simon swirled his wine glass and held it up to the light. There was silence for what seemed like a full minute.

"Maybe you're right, mate. Leave what you have and continue on."

John kept reading until the end. Simon nodded a few times and seemed pleased.

"Lovely," he said. "I'd just like a stronger closing. If I don't get people crying, I haven't done my job."

John took a sip of wine.

"Let me think about it, Simon. I'll type this up and send it to you later."

"No. Let's wrap it up now. We're so close. Paul, what do you think? John was saying what a talent you are. What have you got? Make me cry, my man."

I took a long sip of water.

"Well," I said, "I didn't know the guy, but..."

We sat in silence as I tried to string words together in my head. I began to sweat from my temples.

"Come on, mate," Simon implored with a smile. "I really *need* a good cry. It's been weeks."

"Alright," I said. "You say he was big on charities, never forgot a birthday... What was his name again?"

"Bill," said John. "Bill Burns."

The waiter topped off our wine glasses, buying me time.

"OK," I said, "Here goes. 'I am but one man whose life was graced by the presence of Bill Burns. He touched so very many more. With every card he sent and every charitable donation he made, Bill welcomed the whole world into his home, fed it, clothed it, and sent it back out a better place to be."

Simon bowed his head, a hand over his eyes. John looked back and forth at each of us like we were crazy. I closed.

"Friends will come and friends will go, but if each of is blessed with one like Bill, the world will be a veritable paradise."

I wiped my eyes with my napkin. Simon slowly ran his hand from his eyes down to his chin. He was crying.

"Goddamn, mate. That was beautiful. Did you get that John?"

"Yeah, I got it. By the way, didn't you fuck Bill's wife once?"

"Just once," Simon said through tears.

He reached across the table and shook my hand.

"I think John was right about you, Paul. We'll have to do this again soon."

"Thanks Simon. I'll look forward to it. If you'll excuse me... "

I returned to the bathroom as Simon settled the bill. I had to pee again and I felt like throwing up too, knowing the words I'd shared weren't mine. They were a mash-up of a eulogy my brother Rich had given for my Aunt Bernadette and words my father had written to me when I graduated high school. I had always considered the latter sacred: "If every father could have a son like you, the world would be a veritable paradise." I kicked open a bathroom stall in disgust. I had plagiarized my brother and whored out my dead father to impress an executive, a man I barely knew. I had whored out myself.

"You fucking fraud," I said as I leaned over the toilet. "How could you do that?"

I threw up.

By the time I cleaned myself up and exited the men's room, Simon and John had left the table and were saying goodbye to the hostess. Simon practically licked her arm. I caught up and we walked out onto a humid Sixth Avenue together. The door to Simon's town car was open and frigid air conditioning gushed out.

John had to head home for an appointment with a contractor so he hustled off to hail a cab. I hoped Simon would offer me a ride but he turned and shook my hand.

"A pleasure, Paul. We'll do this again."

I began walking as the car pulled away from the curb and eased into traffic. I kept pace as the limo inched toward a red light ahead. Just as the light turned green, Simon lowered his window.

"One more thing, mate," he shouted, "You'll need to tell me more about this situation with the beach balls."

I stopped walking. The car sped away.

"Fucking John," I said. "That didn't take long."

* * * *

I SNUCK BACK INTO MY OFFICE at 3:00 PM and shut the door. I was greeted by the familiar blinking red light on my phone, but rather than listen to the messages, I merely scrolled through an on-screen read-out of missed calls. If I didn't see any from Mitch or Naomi, I would ignore the voicemails altogether and sleep under my desk. I breathed a sigh of relief when I saw that Mitch hadn't called, nor had he emailed. That's when I remembered.

"Holy shit," I said.

I had forgotten to buy the Del Frisco's gift card. I threw my jacket back on and strode quickly out. Lily waved as I passed.

"Thanks for stopping by, Paul. Come again."

"I'll be back," I said, as I slammed my pelvic bone into a metal mail cart parked in the hallway.

"Cocksucker," I muttered as I turned a corner. I held my side and headed for the elevator bank. A car arrived before I could hit the down button. The doors opened and out stepped Mitch, dressed corporate-casually for the night ahead.

"Paul," he said, "I've been looking for you. Did you get that thing done?"

I hurried past him onto the elevator, panicked that he might pick up on the fact that I'd been drinking.

"Yes Mitch. I got it. I'm just running down to the messenger station to make sure they sent it out."

He looked at me quizzically—*or was it suspiciously?*—as the doors started to close. My harried evasiveness was obvious, but it would have been foolish for me to try to casually fake sobriety face to face.

"Be back soon. See you tonight," I shouted.

Nearing 3:30, I figured traffic wouldn't be too bad, so I once again jumped into a cab on 43rd Street. The backseat was as hot as a sauna so I opened both rear windows and took my jacket off. As we turned onto Sixth Avenue, a sea of cars and cabs clogged the street ahead. I pulled four crumpled singles from my pocket and extended them through the plexiglass.

"Here. Sorry," I said. "I'm an asshole."

By the time I reached the restaurant, bought the gift card, and crossed town to deliver it to the *Tribune*'s reception desk with Mitch's note, the business day was coming to a close. The rented buses to the downtown party would be leaving in just 90 minutes. I wouldn't be napping, but I was at least sobering up a bit as I crisscrossed Midtown. I desperately needed a shower.

Emily didn't seem to want anything to do with me lately. Did I dare use my key to her apartment?

* * * *

THE WORD SPREAD through the party like wildfire. Mitch would be a no-show. As soon as Paige shouted the news in my ear over the thumping Cuban music, I switched from mineral water to a mojito and stopped brooding over John's apparent betrayal of my confidence.

Mitch's eight-year-old had gone over the handlebars of her bicycle that afternoon.

"Eight stitches," Paige screamed. "But she's OK."

"Damn," I shouted back. "Eight more and Thad would be by Mitch's side at the hospital. Where is that asshole?"

"Didn't you hear? He's not making it either."

She high-fived me.

"Holy shit," I said. "What happened?"

"He sprained his ankle," said Paige as she began shaking her shoulders to the music. "White sale at Bloomingdale's."

"What?" I shouted as the deejay raised the volume.

"White sale at Bloomingdale's! He got trampled!"

I felt like I'd won the lottery. I kissed Paige on both cheeks.

"I love you," I shouted.

"I love you too. Let's drink."

"OK!"

I was feeling that happy second wind that only triathletes and problem drinkers get to know. Plus I was fresh from my shower at Emily's. As Paige and I danced—she sexily, I badly—I wondered if I had flushed the toilet before leaving the apartment. Maybe. Maybe not. Fuck it...Emily and I were just about over. She was a secret I wouldn't have to keep much longer. I had five unread emails from her and I was pretty sure that at least one of them was of the "It was fun while it lasted" variety. Still, I considered the remote possibility that she might want to keep things going. If she did, I was open to that too— one more ball to try to keep in the air. As bad as I felt about the affair, it had given me a way to step outside of myself—something I realized I perhaps still needed.

Sally from Media Services danced in between Paige and me, so I peeled back to the far end of the bar to read Emily's emails. Rip the Band-Aid off. I scrolled to the most recent one and prepared myself for the relief and disappointment of the likely end.

I wasn't entirely sure how I would feel, but I was fairly certain Emily would close things out with some degree of warmth. I leaned on the bar and opened the message.

Paul: Please return key to my doorman before I return to States. It's over. Not that it wasn't fun though. Every woman should fuck a savage now and again.

I smirked and got down to convincing myself that I really was relieved. With a day off ahead, the timing was perfect to recommit myself to Diane and Aidan. As I was thinking of something we could all do together, an email from Diane came across. It was the first time she had checked in all day and I smiled at the timing. Things would be OK, I thought. Perhaps she had her own ideas on how we might spend the day.

Paul, Just wanted to give you a heads-up that I'm taking Aidan to the zoo tomorrow. You don't need to come. Meeting my sister to catch up. I'm sure you'll be tired anyway. Please don't make too much noise when you stumble in later. Aidan woke up three times last night.

I stared at the email for a minute, inexplicably read Emily's once more, and powered my phone down. I walked back over to Paige and Sally. Steve Porter from our Detroit office had joined them and was talking animatedly as I approached. He shook my hand but continued the conversation.

"…It was really interesting," he said. "A lot of what she said made sense. And thankfully I didn't draw a card with the grim reaper on it or something."

"Cool, Steve," said Paige. "Glad you had a good reading. A friend recommended her to us. I thought it would be fun."

"What are you guys talking about?" I asked.

Paige pointed to a corner of the restaurant.

"We got a tarot card reader for the night. You have to do it, Paul."

"Sure. She'll tell me I have bad energy and that it will cost ten thousand dollars to clear it."

"I was skeptical too," said Steve, "but she's cool, really."

In truth, I was only pretending to be skeptical. Although I

had never had a tarot reading, I'd heard more than a few tales from trusted sources of scarily accurate readings from mediums and the like. The mystical and spiritual was not something I discounted entirely, but I also knew that for every reputable psychic there were probably a dozen scammers. I eyed the reader from across the room as she flipped cards for a smiling, nodding sales assistant. She looked to be in her early fifties, and while she wore the requisite red gypsy head scarf, she otherwise appeared normal—like she would fit in equally well among suburban housewives or hip urbanites.

"What the hell," I said to Steve. "I'll give it shot. But who needs a drink first?"

We ordered another round of mojitos. The bartender tried to smile, but I could tell he wasn't thrilled to have to crush mint for four more. And I didn't want to wait either.

"Change mine to a Dos Equis," I shouted.

I surveyed the room as I waited. At this point, everyone had heard the news about Mitch and Thad, so the party was getting more happy and raucous by the minute. The dance floor was like a mosh pit, so I held my beer tightly and waded through the revelers. The tarot card lady's small table was set up as far as possible from the deejay booth, but I imagined we would still have to shout to hear each other. She was free and eating a small plate of finger food as I approached. She wiped the corner of her mouth and smiled.

"Hi," she said. "What's your name?"

I put my hands on the back of the chair opposite her.

"Guess."

She tried to hold her smile, but I could tell she was irritated by my answer. Clearly, I wasn't the first person who had said "Guess" to her.

"Just kidding," I added. "I'm Paul."

"Hi Paul. Take a seat. Relax."

I wondered why she would tell me to relax. Did she say that to everyone? Or did I strike her as tense? In spite of everything that had happened that day, I oddly felt more relaxed than I had in months. I leaned back in the chair and affected the most casual air I could summon. We made small talk for a few seconds, but she could see by the way I eyed the cards that I was eager to get started.

"Ready?" she asked.

"Hit me," I said, as if she were a blackjack dealer.

She handed me the deck and told me to shuffle it a few times. I took a long sip of my beer and placed it on the table. I figured that whatever I was thinking about as I shuffled would be important, but my thoughts were a jumble: Mitch and the beach ball, Simon and what he wanted to know about the beach ball, whoring out my father, John's loose lips, the presentation I had to work on, what Diane might say to her bitchy sister about me, the fact that I'd never see Emily naked again, family phone calls I hadn't returned, dry cleaning I'd forgotten to pick up.

"Very thorough shuffle," said the tarot card lady as she reached for the deck.

She spread the cards out and told me to choose six. I tapped my choices in a back and forth pattern.

As she began to flip them over, Paige appeared over my shoulder and handed me a shot.

"Tequila!" she shouted. "Didn't want you to miss out!"

"Thanks," I said, knocking it back and chasing it with my beer.

I had hardly eaten since the wine-soaked lunch, so I felt my heavy buzz returning. The second wind was quickly transitioning to a second slog. Paige shouted a "Sorry for interrupting!" as she left, but the tarot card lady didn't respond. In fact, she seemed slightly annoyed—which made me feel annoyed for Paige's sake. It wasn't like we were discussing a biopsy here. Sure, I thought, it's nice that she was taking her work seriously, but at the end of the day *you're a fucking tarot card reader, lady—and probably a crook.* I wondered how much money she was taking us for. She probably didn't even have a real job. But why should she? She could make a living off Carlyle Nash and our stupid six-figure parties alone. My mood was turning sour. I looked around and saw how much fun people were having at the bar and on the dance floor.

Let's get this shit over with.

"OK," she said. "There's a lot here."

She folded her hands and straightened as if she were about to address the United Nations.

I should just get up.

"This is an exciting time for you," she began.

"You think?" I said as I extended my arms in sweeping reference to the party around us. "There's a chicken fight on the dance floor and I could be in the next one."

She inhaled and exhaled deeply and looked down at the cards. Before her lay a combination of knights, moons, fools, Formula One drivers, whatever. Skepticism had taken me hostage.

"It's an exciting time," she repeated, "because many new people have come into your life and others will too."

"Yep."

"And this is what you've wanted. But as exciting as life is— with all the success that comes with it—you need to remember what's really important. Maintain balance."

I could get the same advice from a multivitamin ad.

"Yes," I said. "Balance is critical. I should be taking notes here."

Paige dropped off another shot and darted away.

"You're the best, Paige!" I shouted after her.

"That's about it," said the tarot card lady.

"What? That's it? You said there was a lot here. Don't I get to know if I'll win the lottery?"

She sipped from a cup of coffee.

"That's not what the tarot is about. And it looks like you'd be happier at the bar anyway."

Oh, so this is how it's gonna be.

"Well," I said, "Of course I'd be happier at the bar, but I'm sure you're being paid very well tonight, so I'd like a full reading, Esmeralda."

"I don't like to do readings for people who are clearly... distracted."

I raised my shot glass high, held it for a beat, and downed it. A few drops escaped down the side of my chin.

"I may be 'distracted,' but not so much that I can't put an end to the great word-of-mouth you get around the Carlyle Nash building."

We stared each other down for a few seconds.

"Fine," she said. "The cards are saying one more thing."

"And what's that?"

"You should watch your family," she said with a smile. "It could be falling apart."

I reached for my beer but it was empty.

"You know," I said, "she was the one who pursued me."

"Of course she was. I'm afraid our time is up."

I noticed that the card to the far right had a picture of a man lying face down on the ground. Multiple swords were sticking out of his lifeless body.

"What does that one mean?"

"Look it up," she said.

"Fuck off, lady."

I stood up and knocked my bottle to the floor. It shattered at the feet of three colleagues in conversation.

"What the fuck, Paul!"

"What's the matter with you?"

"Dude!"

"I'm sorry, I'm sorry," I said, "It was an accident."

"Dude...come on!"

"I'm really sorry."

I looked down at the tarot card lady.

"I'm sorry. I shouldn't have—"

She said something in response, but all I could make out was "family." The music was louder than ever. As the room seemed to tilt, I searched for an exit. ▪

CHAPTER SIXTEEN

A Savage
at *Bellwether*

(2006)

I WAS LOOKING AT A PRINTOUT of Aidan's 20-week ultra-sound when Emily called me from The Four Seasons. She was finally back in the States after a few months of reporting in Iraq. Over the course of that time—from our first flirtation at the *Bellwether* sales meeting dinner to phone sex at the office after an air raid in Baghdad—our e-relationship had gone from "Nice photo, beautiful eyes" to "I'm going to fuck you like Elvis on Priscilla."

With *Bellwether* humming along, Michael departing, and Mitch transitioning to the nascent *World* launch, my workload had been bearable. But I was still keeping late hours to pursue my passionate virtual affair. Diane didn't suspect a thing; she had been wrapped up in third-trimester nesting for weeks. I knew full well that I was the worst husband on the planet, but I couldn't stop myself. Never before in my life had a woman been attracted to me for purely physical reasons. I thought about Emily to the point of distraction. And yet, I still wasn't sure if I could go through with it. I imagined my best self ending things at lunch before anything could happen. If only.

"Meet me in the bar…now," she said.

"I have an eleven-thirty meeting and then I'm off for the day. I'll head straight there."

"Say what you wrote to me in your last email."

"I don't remember, Emily."

"Of course, you remember," she cooed. "Please. Say it."

I cleared my throat.

"I'm gonna take you like a fucking savage."

She moaned softly.

"Don't order a drink when you get here."

"Maybe. See you in a bit."

My hands were shaking as I hung up the phone.

I had lied about the 11:30 meeting because I had plans to meet John for a quick drink at noon to discuss his still dangling job offer. I needed that drink now to calm myself, so I dialed him early. He picked up on the first ring.

"Yeah, I'm ready," he said.

"See you over there."

As I put my jacket on and walked toward the elevator, my Blackberry vibrated. It was an email from Thad Bellows in Los Angeles. He had been Mitch's first hire for *World*, which meant he'd be relocating to New York. The email read:

Hello Paul. I hope you're well. As you know, Mitch is putting his launch team together for World. He has already begun seeing candidates for the Marketing Director position. It will be very competitive. It has been suggested to me that you get on his calendar next week if you'd like to be considered for the role.

I smiled. I had made the right move in not pursuing the job immediately after the announcement of the launch— even though Michael had told me I would be a top candidate. By waiting, I had forced Mitch's hand and gotten him to effectively reveal that he thought me worthy of the job. I was being invited to pursue it, but perhaps I was being pursued too. I still couldn't be entirely sure, but at least I now knew I wouldn't be setting myself up for the disappointment of being told I wasn't ready. I knew I was ready. Now I knew Mitch did too.

John had beaten me to the Millennium and was a third of the way down on a Bloody Mary. He smiled as I ordered the same.

"Don't tell me," he said. "You're finally coming to work for me."

"You haven't even made me an official offer yet."

"Just tell me you're coming and then I'll give you a deal. Don't worry. It'll be solid. I can get as much out of Simon as needed."

"I'll still need to think about it."

"For Christ's sake, Paul. Don't tell me you're going to chase Mitch to *World*. What is it with you and him?"

I shifted uncomfortably on my barstool.

"I'm not here to talk about my next move, John. I'm just having a quick drink before lunch."

He pushed a menu at me.

"My lunch canceled. Let's eat here."

"I can't," I said as I grabbed a few pretzels. "I'm meeting someone."

"Who?"

"Just an old friend."

John sat upright.

"Wait a minute," he said. "She's here, isn't she? You're gonna do it. You're gonna fuck her. Unbelievable."

I put my head in my hands as he began his lecture.

"Listen, as I've said before, be careful with this shit. I've seen it fuck up a lot of lives."

I guzzled my drink and got up.

"I know, I know," I said. "I'm not even sure if I'll go through with it. But I have to go."

"Already? Come on. Have one more and think about it."

"I can't," I said, backpedaling out. "I'll call you tomorrow."

"Call me later," John shouted.

I hailed a cab and headed uptown. The backseat TV screen was blaring the local news. I hit the mute button to gather my thoughts but the touch screen wasn't working, so I rolled down the window to drown out the audio. The sidewalks were jammed with pedestrians. The first ones I noticed were a husband and wife pushing a baby stroller. I would have asked myself if I was ready to be a father, but the answer was becoming clearer with each passing city block. I turned my attention back to the screen as I unwrapped a stick of gum.

We pulled up to The Four Seasons and my heartbeat quickened. As a doorman held the door, I swallowed my gum and breathed deeply. I lingered in the lobby for a minute and took a last look at my Blackberry. All was quiet.

Emily was the only person at the bar. She was reading *Bellwether* when I entered, but she saw me from afar. She stood up and smiled as I approached. Her brown hair had grown out a bit and was now styled in a bob. She was dressed more like an executive than a writer this time: white satin blouse, two top buttons undone, above-the-knee charcoal skirt over black pumps.

I put my right hand lightly on her waist and kissed her cheek.

"At long last," she said as she tugged at my tie. "You know...I won't hold a stumbling, awkward first kiss against you. If you're brave, that is."

The bartender had been quietly cutting limes directly in front of us. He looked up for just a second before politely moving away to wash his knife in the sink. I put both hands around Emily's waist.

"Thanks for lowering and raising the bar in one sentence," I said.

She smiled and wrapped her arms around my neck. She pressed her body hard against mine. We kissed as if we'd trained for the moment. We ended with a long look into each other's eyes. I broke the gaze first.

"Can I get a drink now?" I asked.

"My place. Private bar. Come, savage."

She palmed my erection through my pants and we kissed again. My entire world receded from view.

* * * *

I GOT HOME AT JUST PAST EIGHT. Diane was sitting on the floor of the near-finished nursery looking at carpet swatches. I somehow considered it virtuous that I'd had only one drink since noon.

"Hi," I said as I bent to kiss her. "How are you feeling?"

"I feel good. Were you smoking a cigar?"

I hadn't smoked a cigar. But after leaving Emily's apartment, I'd headed straight to the Nat Sherman cigar shop on 42nd Street and sat in their smoking room for a good hour in an apparently successful attempt to mask Emily's scent.

"No," I said casually, "but I met John after work to catch up. He needed to buy a gift for his brother, so I went with him to Nat Sherman. You can barely see through the smoke in that place."

Diane extended her hand and I helped her up.

"Where are things at?" she asked. "Did he make you the offer?"

"Oh. Well, no...not yet. I mean...there are other factors right now."

"What are you talking about, Paul? You're going to go to Corporate."

"Mitch wants to meet with me about *World*."

Diane threw up her hands.

"For God's sake, Paul. You can't be serious. Didn't you once say that the news category was dying? But I guess not if Mitch the Miracle Worker is in it, am I right?"

"That's actually true, Diane. If anyone can remake the category for the next generation, it's Mitch."

"'If anyone can remake the category for the next generation, it's Mitch.' Do you know how pathetic that sounds, Paul?"

"Diane, please. This is my career and it has to be my decision. I know what I'm doing."

"I don't think you do, Paul. When the baby comes, the last thing I need is for you to be obsessing over where you stand with Mitch."

"Can I just take a shower? I haven't even thought it all through yet. But I won't do anything without talking to you first, OK?"

The phone rang and Diane brushed past me to answer it.

I sagged in the center of the nursery and thought of Emily.

"Stay, savage," she had pleaded as I left her lying at the end of her king bed—naked, glistening, and clutching a pillow.

* * * *

B Y THE TIME I got out of the shower, Diane had gone to bed. It was 9:00 PM. We had recently moved our computer and office equipment from their former location in the nursery to a corner of our finished basement. My body was drained as I descended into the cool darkness, but my mind was racing. I turned on the overhead lamp above the desk and settled in. I liked the dim seclusion of the new spot. I logged into my private email for communicating with Emily: SavageMktr9@hotmail.com.

Paul—Missing you. Had to move up my departure to Tuesday. Must see you Monday. Yes?

To the right of the computer sat a framed photo of me and Diane on our honeymoon. We were standing at the end of a dock. My arms enveloped her from behind. I remember propping the Canon up on a post, setting the timer, and sprinting into the shot. I looked happy and a bit thinner. Diane always felt it wasn't her best photo, but I loved it, so she always placed it somewhere I could see it.

"God forgive me," I said as I closed my eyes.

When I opened them, my right hand was resting on the keyboard, with the index finger already on Y.

Yes.

Emily responded within seconds.

Good savage. Sweet dreams.

I closed out the program and logged into my work email. Thad had sent a follow-up:

Paul: I neglected to mention that Mitch has asked all Marketing Director candidates to submit a position paper on New Media. It must run anywhere from 3,500 to 5,000 words and represent your thoughts on how digital innovations will impact our industry. Take no more than one week to prepare it, and submit it to Mitch's assistant at least 48 hours before your scheduled meeting. Any questions, let me know. —Thad

My right knee began bouncing up and down. I immediately created a new folder on the desktop and labeled it "New Media Paper." I opened a Word document and typed the word "Outline."

If there was one thing I knew for sure about my nameless internal competitors for the position it was that they couldn't match my speed. Give Carlyle Nashers a week on a project, and they'll use every minute of it. I had long taken a different approach. While I could bitch about sales reps as much as anyone else, I always knew that they were on the front lines and that it was my job to get them what they needed fast. The less notice the better, in fact. As far back as grammar school, I had been creating impossible deadlines for myself: banging out night-before book reports amid big family chaos. *You should have started that sooner*, my mother would yell.

This paper, I vowed, would be in Mitch's in-box by sun-up. I imagined my competitors out at a movie, watching TV, or snug in bed. Lazy, privileged bastards. And I thought of Leo Breslin, tattooed Korean War vet and deli manager, shouting in my 16-year-old face.

You think this is some kind of country club, Cavanaugh? Move your ass.

* * * *

BELLWETHER'S NEWLY ANNOUNCED Publisher made the rounds the next day, but I hardly cared. Carlyle Nash had done its standard shuffle: move a veteran from one title—in this case our golf magazine—into the vacated top job at another, slide another exec over to replace him or her, fire a third Publisher who wasn't getting it done, and bring in a newcomer to shake things up. The building quaked for a few days and Lou Lamont had material for two weeks' worth of columns. If there was anything the Moreland family loved, it was publicity.

My phone rang, but I didn't recognize the name. I picked up right before it could go to voicemail.

"Hello, this is Paul."

"Hi Paul. This is Naomi Lee. I'm Mitch Blake's new assistant. Mitch would like to know if you're free to come by his office."

"Now?" I said as I stood up.

"Yes, is that possible? This is his only opening today."

"Yes, of course. I'll be right there."

"Great," said Naomi, "We're on the twenty-fifth floor."

I could hear the new Publisher, Julia Barr, circulating among the cube dwellers: "So nice to meet you. I look forward to working with you..." She was getting closer and closer to my office so I shut the door, fixed my tie, and put on my brown suit jacket. Unfortunately, it was my rainy-day suit—I had worn my best interview suit for Emily. It would have to do.

I exited and turned the corner. Ten feet ahead stood Julia and Lois Knight, who was making the introductions.

"And here's Paul," said Lois. "Paul is—"

I grabbed Julia's hand and shook it.

"Great to meet you, but I'm afraid I have to run to a meeting."

She looked at me icily. I wasn't kissing the ring.

As I dashed to the elevators, I noted I'd be off to a rocky start with her if I didn't nail the interview with Mitch.

The 25th floor had been vacant ever since the company killed off *Sharp*, an ill-advised men's shopping magazine. The sprawling space had a ghostly feel as I traversed it, but as I neared the partitioned-off far end, where I heard voices and the sounds of activity, I felt the energy of an ambitious start-up. Three sales aces were working the phones from a row of open-plan stations, temps were unpacking boxes, oversized mock-ups of possible *World* logos were Scotch-taped to the walls. The young woman sitting outside the large corner office had to be Naomi. She saw me approaching and stood up.

"Paul?"

"Hi, yes," I said. "Nice to meet you, Naomi."

"Nice to meet you too. You can go right in."

Mitch was sitting on a temporary couch left over from *Sharp*. He was uncharacteristically dressed down in jeans, loafers, and a polo shirt. Looking the part of an entrepreneur, I supposed. He stood up and we shook hands.

"Hello Mitch," I said.

"Paul. Thanks for coming down on short notice."

"No problem at all, Mitch."

He walked behind his desk and picked up a copy of my position paper. He held it up.

"But something tells me you don't have a problem with short notice, do you?"

I smiled proudly.

"No I don't, Mitch. In fact I—"

"But here's the problem. I don't agree with a thing in it."

I sat down, but he was still standing. He glanced down at me. I stood back up.

"Well, I, I think… Would you like to talk about it?"

"Sit down, Paul."

I sat down and breathed deeply.

Holy shit. Don't blow this.

"Listen," he said, crossing to sit on a windowsill, "this is well written and well sourced—a lot like your *Bellwether* work—but it's a bit counterintuitive."

"Well, I just think that the industry is in a headlong rush to embrace something we don't understand well enough. For example, in the section where I discuss how traditional media is—"

Mitch raised his hand.

"It's OK. Relax, Paul. I'm not overly concerned about it, because if you accept this job, our messaging on new media or anything else will be made clear early on. The question is can you execute the message? That's the job."

I cleared my throat.

"Am I being *offered* the job?"

He crossed back to his desk and sat down, just as the phone began to ring. He looked out to Naomi to see who was calling.

"It's Lou Lamont," said Naomi, "from the *New York Tribune*."

Mitch looked up at me.

"I have to take this," he said. "But expect a call from HR."

He motioned for Naomi to enter. As I stood, stunned, he spoke into the phone while jotting something on a sticky note. He handed it to Naomi and looked up at me quizzically, as if to say "What are you still doing here?"

He looked back down and I shuffled out.

For the next few hours, I sat in my office replaying the meeting over and over in my head. *Expect a call from HR.* He had said the words, so why was I worried the call might not come? Or if it did come, could it be to tell me I was out of the running? Perhaps he was right then being blown away by another candidate's paper.

Following a restless night, however, the next morning, the call that proved my fears unfounded came. By the end of another work day spent dodging calls from Emily, I was holding in my hands an official outline of the offer: Marketing Director of *World* Magazine, more money than I'd ever made, and a coveted spot on Mitch Blake's management team. I accepted before I left for the night.

I strung the story out to Diane for a week—to give her the idea that I was tortured by the decision. She was angry that I chose against her wishes, but she also admitted that there are some private goals a person just can't abandon. She would pray for the best.

"I hope you can forgive me," I said.

"I can forgive anything, Paul," she said with a sigh. "Except cheating."

"Never, Diane."

As for John, I felt sure he would forgive me too and even understand. He had said himself that Simon had been his own white whale at one time.

A few days after I accepted the offer, I was packing up my *Bellwether* files when Naomi dropped off a gift box. Wine, it looked like. I sat down and opened it. Inside was a bottle of Dom Perignon. The card read:

Paul—Glad you're on board. Congrats, Mitch

I leaned back in my chair and smiled. All of my hard work had paid off. And the best part was that Mitch's decision appeared to be all about merit, about *the work*. As I admired the bottle in my hands, I concluded that production was the only thing that mattered to Mitch. He perhaps hadn't even considered, cared about, or noticed anything else in my personal makeup. There was no need to look back anymore. *Just focus on the task ahead*, I told myself. *Bellwether* was a part of my past.

I dashed off an email to him, expressing my appreciation for the opportunity and my thanks for the champagne. He emailed back immediately:

My pleasure. Drink it now though. You'll need to be sober for this. ▪

PART II: 2007-2008

The Ten of Swords

CHAPTER SEVENTEEN

Friday the 13th
(2007)

I FELT LIKE THE LAST MAN ON EARTH as I wept at my desk on Friday afternoon. Every other staffer had taken advantage of the two free days off that Mitch had given us, but not me. I sat amidst a trove of attack research I had done that morning for my *Globalist* presentation, letting the tears come. I had started off fresh and ready after sleeping away most of a Thursday and enjoying a civil dinner with Diane. She had complained that Mitch "should have just given you Friday off, too," but I'd caught a smile when I'd told her the tarot card lady had seen nothing but joy and abundance ahead.

Just past noon, however, when she had called me with the bad news, my focus had shattered. My Uncle Frank had died.

"I'm sorry, Paul. I know how much he meant to you. Your mom said the wake and funeral are on Tuesday and Wednesday."

"Are they bringing him here?" I asked. "Or is it in Philadelphia?"

"Philadelphia. Maybe you can take your mother. I'll have to stay here with Aidan."

"OK. Do me a favor. His girlfriend's phone number is in my

address book in the top drawer of my dresser: Elaine Macey. Email it to me when you have a minute."

"I will. Come home early."

"I'll try."

I turned to my bulletin board. I reached for the sticky note that had been there for weeks. It read *Call Uncle Frank* and included the phone number for his hospital room. I stared at it for a few seconds and then threw it in the trash. I tried to convince myself that he was the type of person who would have hated a teary last phone call. He would have just told me he was fine and that I should get back to work. I wasn't sure I believed it. Whatever the case, he was—as they say—in a better place now. And if my father had been looking down on me in shame these past two years, Uncle Frank would be by his side now saying, "Give the kid a break, Jack. It was just a fling. It's over."

I was staring blankly at my computer screen when a *Tribune* email alert popped up. The subject line read: World *on the Ropes?* I clicked it open to Lou Lamont's Friday column. The piece documented advertiser flight from the magazine and mentioned not just the IBM pullout but rumors about three other major clients who had soured on *World* after the bloated premiere issue and tales of dysfunction on the editorial side—rumors even I hadn't heard yet.

Clearly the Del Frisco's gift card hadn't arrived in time to convince him to possibly hold the story. Had I simply bought the card and sent it over instead of having lunch with Simon and John, maybe he would have killed it. Would Mitch figure out that it was my fault? Or worse, would he think I was deliberately sabotaging his efforts and then connect that to the missing beach ball? Maybe Simon had already begun spreading the word that I had the beach ball—if in fact John had told him specifically that I did have it. I desperately needed to speak to John, but he had yet to respond to the angry voice mail I had left him.

I put my face in my hands and moaned.

What the hell do I do now?

Tears began to flow again.

I'm sorry, Uncle Frank.

Suddenly I heard a loud crash that launched me out of my chair in panic. *What the hell is that?* It sounded like a file cabinet falling over in somebody's office, but the offices were all supposed to be empty.

I wiped my eyes, walked quietly to my open door, tiptoed out into Lily's workstation and climbed up on her chair to peer over her overhead cabinets. From that position, I could see above all the cubicles, all the way to the other end of the floor. The crash had come from a cubicle about 30 yards away. Whoever was in there seemed to be bent over now cleaning up the mess. I watched and waited until the person got up. He stood with his back turned, but I recognized him right away.

It was Mitch. He was wearing his fencing gear, all except for the mask.

He's looking for the beach ball. I know it.

As he began inspecting the next cubicle, I scurried back into my office, closed the door gently, and just stood there. My heart was racing. My door didn't have a lock.

Is he going to check every cubicle? And every...office? Shit, shit, shit.

I could hear him working his way closer and closer. Soon enough, he was right outside at Lily's desk. A friend had recently sent her one of those awful musical birthday cards, and Mitch opened it.

I could hear the two Chipmunk-sounding characters trading knock-knock, you're-getting-old jokes before warbling a painful rendition of the Beatles' "They Say It's Your Birthday" song. Mitch seemed to like it: he chuckled and played it again. And again.

Jesus, I thought he had a more refined sense of humor.

I noted for the thousandth time how little I really knew about this man. As he opened the card once more, I circled back to my desk and sat down. I grabbed a pencil and legal pad and started scribbling random notes while looking at the doorknob. It began to turn. I tried to look natural.

"Whoa," said Mitch, taking a step back, "Paul...I didn't know you'd be here. I was looking for a, uh—"

"It's OK, Mitch," I said, "What can I do for you?"

"What are you doing here today, Paul?"

I motioned to the mound of research on my desk.

"Just trying to get the *Globalist* presentation done by Monday. I know you're waiting on that."

Mitch sat down in one of my chairs. It was the first time he'd ever done that, and he looked tired and a bit smaller as I looked down on him. The perspective seemed to humanize him—even in fencing gear. I assumed he had come straight from a lesson at his fencing center or fencing emporium or whatever it was called, but I wasn't going to ask.

"Just have it ready for the offsite on Wednesday," he said. "Go home."

"The offsite?"

"Thad didn't send the email yet?" I began to panic. Uncle Frank's funeral was on Wednesday.

"No Mitch," I said. "Do you mean this Wednesday?"

"Yes. We need to get the management team together for a strategy session on turning the skittish clients around. Unfortunately, Lou Lamont's messenger station never gave him the Del Frisco's card—but thanks for handling that. Anyway, we'll head up to the Mohonk Mountain House on Tuesday night and then hunker down all day Wednesday."

I breathed a small sigh of relief that the gift card hadn't blown up on me, but I swallowed hard at the news of the offsite. As Mitch leaned back and examined a small cut on his hand, I knew that if ever there was a time to deliver the news about my Uncle Frank, it was now. I imagined Mitch would say, "I'm sorry, Paul. I understand. Have a safe trip to Philadelphia." But, then again, he might say, "Your Uncle? Really Paul?" Shit, he might even say "Uncles die, Paul. It's what they do. See you at the offsite."

I couldn't be sure. My throat tightened.

"Mohonk," I said.

"Yes, it's perfect for this. No TVs. No distractions...and no tequila."

I looked down.

"I heard about it," Mitch continued. "When the cat's away..."

"Sorry Mitch. Yeah, things got a little crazy at the party, but..."

He stood up to leave.

"Well," he said, "Let's try to stay focused, OK?"

"I will, Mitch."

He pointed at my research.

"And as I said, leave that for Monday. But I do want to see something good at Mohonk."

"OK. I think you'll like it. I'm going at them hard."

He shut the door behind him as he left.

* * * *

A S I APPROACHED Emily's building to return her key later that afternoon, I thought back over our run. Since our first meeting two years earlier, I had managed to keep the relationship a secret to everyone but John. Although an affair of that length could normally be categorized as more than just a fling, the ratio of phone sex to real sex had run roughly four to one. When she was in town, we would start with dinner in a discreet restaurant. We would eat quickly—not only because she couldn't keep her foot off my crotch, but also because a Rhodes Scholar can only bear so much conversation with, well, a man who didn't quite make the cut.

"Yes," I once said, "I do like coriander. It's durable."

She stifled a laugh.

"Durable? Coriander is a spice, Paul."

I smiled.

"I knew that. It's durable. Stands up to intense heat."

She laughed.

"You're one job removed from slinging hash somewhere, aren't you?"

"All work is noble, Emily."

"Yes. That's what people who work around cockroaches tell themselves."

"Speaking of durable, did you know that roaches—"

"Get the check, savage."

Then it would be back to her place for a few hours of "working late." A day later she'd be off to the next global hot spot for several weeks or even months of reporting. It worked well for a while...until a worldly journalist for the *Irish Independent* proved just savage enough to take my place.

I approached the lobby desk. Gary the Doorman greeted me with his standard wry smile. I slapped the key down on the marble top like a man paying an overdue bar tab.

He looked at it and laughed.

"So you finally decided to stop putting the wood to the witch?"

"Not exactly."

He smiled knowingly.

"I've seen him already," he said. "If it makes you feel any better, he's a pompous asshole. Gives the Irish a bad name."

I reached across to shake his hand.

"It really is for the better," I said. "But let's get a beer some time. You can tell me who she's fucking that week."

"You bet, man. Now go home to whatever you've got there. I'm sure she's better than this one."

"She is. Take it easy, man."

"You too, brother."

As I headed straight for Penn Station, I realized that Diane had never emailed me the phone number for Uncle Frank's girlfriend. I didn't want her to know I'd left the office early—I had to keep up the workday ruse, plus make one more stop near home—so I emailed her a reminder instead of calling. By the time I reached Cold Spring Harbor at around 4:00 PM, she still hadn't responded. I pointed the Malibu in the direction of Hicksville to pick up the letter my friend from Florida had sent to my old address.

* * * *

KEITH HAD LET THE PLACE GO over the years. The lawn, if it could be called one, was a mass of crabgrass, wild flowers, and bare patches of earth. The aluminum siding on the house was badly in need of a power wash, and the gutters were overflowing with last fall's leaves. The three spare truck tires that had always been stacked just to the right of the garage were still there, cracked and weathered. Sticking up from the center of the stack was a Wiffle bat and a mud-covered push broom. A detached and damaged screen door was leaning horizontally against the tires. As I knocked on the partially open front door, I noticed that the second mailbox for the upstairs tenant still had a faded white sticker with my last name on it, but the letters had been crossed out. In the narrow space above, the name "Loomis" had been scrawled, but it too had a line through it.

Keith opened the door with his foot. His right hand was heavily bandaged and he was holding a box of frozen hamburgers with his left.

"Hey Keith," I said. "Long time, man."

"Holy shit. You're finally here. Get in. Help me with this."

"With what?"

"With this fucking box of burgers. I can't get it open. Come to the kitchen."

We passed through the living room on the way. The woman's touch that had once been present appeared long gone. On one wall was a massive oil painting of a motorcycle. On another hung a neon Miller Genuine Draft sign that looked like it had come from the window of a bar or convenience store. The sign gave off an audible hum and was plugged into an overloaded power strip crowded with plugs for an amplifier, a Shop-Vac, and a tall lamp without a shade. The bay window's moldy drapes looked permanently closed.

"What happened to your hand?" I asked.

Keith handed me a carving knife.

"I got a speeding ticket. Punched my windshield after the cop wouldn't even look at my PBA card. Asshole."

"With a PBA card, it's all in the way you present it."

"Yeah, I should have presented it right up his ass."

I opened the box of hamburgers. The plastic bag inside was covered in frost.

I brushed it off, tore the package open, and handed it over.

"Fresh from the butcher," I said.

"You want one?" Keith asked as he violently bashed the stuck-together patties on the counter.

"Sure," I replied, "Maybe."

"Maybe? What the fuck? Do you or don't you?"

"OK. I'll have one. They look delicious."

"Grab a couple of beers from the fridge and come out back."

We stepped out onto his splintered deck and Keith ignited his propane grill. I looked up at the staircase leading to the old apartment. I wondered who was in there now and if they had maintained it with the same care Diane always had.

"Who's upstairs?" I asked.

"Nobody. My mother for a bit, but she kicked. Then I had a guy up there who paid steady for a while, but he became a fucking meth head. Bye-bye."

"So where's Renee?"

"Oh man," said Keith as he wire-brushed smoking black muck from the grill. "She's long gone. Fucked my buddy, so I booted her."

"Wow. Sorry."

"Don't be. The only thing I miss is her paycheck. I'm way behind on this shithole. How's your lady? You two still making googly eyes at each other all the time?"

"She's good. We're good."

He dropped two patties on the red-hot grates.

"Remember the time I caught you two fucking in my shed?"

I knew he was going to bring that up.

He pointed a spatula at me and laughed.

"You had a whole apartment up there but you had to have sex next to my snow blower."

"We were crazy back then," I said. "Hey, by the way, where's the letter you called me about?"

"It's on the shelf above the kitchen sink. Go ahead."

I went back in, found the envelope, and opened it. My old friend from *Blowback* was coming to town and wanted to get together. We had lost track of each other after Diane and I moved, so all he had was the Hicksville address. I checked when he'd be here. The date had already passed. I put the card in my pocket and lingered in the kitchen for a few minutes, checking emails. Still nothing from Diane. John was frustratingly offline too. There was one new message, however. My brother Rich had emailed about travel plans to Philadelphia. He closed with: *I guess it's going to take a death in the family for you to show your face.*

Keith brought the hamburgers in, and we had a second beer and caught up for another half hour. I had killed enough time, so I wished him well and headed home.

When I arrived, Diane's car wasn't in the driveway. I figured she must be running errands without her phone. My neighbor Fred was doing yard work across the street as I approached my front steps. I waved to him but he just looked back down at his lawn. One too many declined invites on my part, I supposed.

The first thing I noticed when I entered the house was the note. It was sitting in the center of the kitchen island. I knew instinctively that it wasn't a grocery list. I pulled out a kitchen stool, sat down slowly, and closed my eyes. *Please tell me she didn't find out about Emily, especially now that it's over.*

I waited a minute, picked up the note, and began reading.

Paul, Writing this note is like an out-of-body experience. But we both know why it's come to this. How I could go from being the center of your world to someone who feels like she's just in your way is a mystery to me. What saddens me even more is that Aidan has barely made it into your world.

I had planned on discussing time away from each other next week (certainly not until after your Uncle's funeral) but when I found this card in your dresser, I simply couldn't stay...

"Card," I said aloud. "What card? Emily never gave me a card."

It was then I noticed something else on the table that had been underneath the note. I recognized the card instantly:

SUMMER ACHIEVEMENT AWARD
WORLD *OFFICE CLOSED THIS THURSDAY AND FRIDAY*
ENJOY!

I finished reading Diane's note.

...After all our arguments over long hours, late nights, missed appointments, you lie to me about a day off. A man in his right mind would have jumped at the chance to spend a Friday with his wife and son, but not you. You went to an empty office. You're not in your right mind, Paul.

I don't want this to be forever. I just want you to finally see what you've done to us. Maybe some time alone will help you do that. All I can do is hope and pray that it does.

I'll be at my sister's for a few days, but don't call. I'll call you when I'm ready. And I won't tell your mother—at least not yet. I leave that to you. When you get back from Philadelphia, please make arrangements to stay somewhere else for a while. Aidan needs to be in his home. —Diane ▪

CHAPTER EIGHTEEN

Monday Early
(2007)

I F HE WERE IN MY SHOES, I told myself, Uncle Frank would do the same thing. Following a weekend during which my emotions had swung from despair to rage, I had called my mother and told her I wouldn't be going to the funeral. A mass card and flowers were en route. Thankfully, her Depression-era outlook had always been that anyone could lose their job at any time, so she told me to go to the offsite.

"You see?" I shouted at an imaginary Diane. "My own mother understands the importance of this better than you."

I knew that many of my siblings would curse me, but I couldn't think about them just then.

I woke up early Monday morning on an inflatable mattress in the middle of my old apartment. Keith had reacted like he'd won the lottery when I'd called him on Sunday with the news that Diane was gone and I needed a place.

"Fuckin' A," he said, "I know you'll pay."

The bathroom and shower were surprisingly clean. He had lugged a power washer up the stairs to blast the surfaces. The force had knocked out a ceiling tile and the toilet paper holder, but that was the extent of the damage.

As I got ready for work, I made a mental list of the things I had to do: finish my *Globalist* presentation, track down John to finally find out what he had told Simon regarding the beach ball, and ask Paige just how bad my drunken exit from the party had been. Not your traditional to-do list.

When I opened the shower curtain, I half-expected our old Steak-umm-loving cat to be curled up on the bath rug. But she was long gone too. I thought back to the day Diane had broken down and let Bridget in the apartment. They were lying on the couch together when I walked in, both purring happily.

"You know," Diane had said, "they choose who they're going to love. Like I chose you."

After a minute or two, I realized I was standing motionless in the shower, all dried off. I slicked my hair back, dressed quickly, and headed to the train station.

* * * *

JOHN WOULD TYPICALLY ARRIVE at his office by 8:00 AM, but I knew it might be tough to get a few minutes with him. One of the first things he had taught me back at *Bellwether* was to frontload meetings before noon so liquid lunches could run long. Nevertheless, I went to see him at 8:15. When I walked in without knocking he was thankfully alone but on the phone with his son.

"That's a shitty offer," he said. "That company has deep pockets. Hold out, Max."

He waved to me and pointed to a chair.

"Listen to your old man," he continued. "Do not accept. They will respect you if you ask for more money. Call me after you do. I have to go."

He looked at me.

"Have I told you how much I hate your fucking hair like that? You look like you work at Carlyle Nash."

"I do work at Carlyle Nash. You didn't call me back."

"I was just about to. Madelyn and I went away for the long weekend. No work. That was the deal."

"Why the hell did you tell Simon what I told you about the beach ball?"

He jerked his head back.

"He asked you about it? When?"

"Right after lunch. He shouted from his limo that he wants to hear more. What the fuck? Did you tell him when I was in the bathroom throwing up?"

"You threw up at Del Frisco's?"

"Yeah, whatever. Why did you tell him?"

John stood up and shut the door.

"I didn't tell him anything, Paul. He asked me if you were the guy who told Jennie about the beach balls. *She* told him."

"Jennie?" I said. "Who the fuck—"

"*Jennieeeee*, his assistant. Don't you remember? Kite flying? Captain *World*? Johnnie Walker Blue?"

"Holy shit."

John laughed.

"*You* told her about the beach balls, you drunk fucking idiot. And she told Simon."

"Oh for God's sake," I said as I put my face in my hands.

"But listen. He doesn't know that you kept one. And I didn't tell him either. All he knows is that Mitch recalled them. So I guess that's all you told Jennie too."

"But why was she even talking to Simon about it?"

John sighed and shook his head.

"They talk about everything, Paul. He's fucking her."

"I'm a complete moron."

John began gathering things for a meeting.

"Hey," he said. "What are you doing tonight?"

"Nothing. Diane left me."

"No way. She found out?"

"Not about Emily. I'll explain tonight... What is tonight?"

"Simon is presenting the company's new ad campaign to pretty much every media buyer and trade reporter in the business. It's at Radio City. You can be my guest. Madelyn can't make it."

"OK," I said.

When I got back to my office, I shut the door and buried myself in more *Globalist* opposition research—not only because the presentation would make or break me given both my behavior at the party and the importance of the offsite, but because I needed to push Diane, Emily, and Uncle Frank as far from my mind as possible.

I directed every ounce of anger, stress, and frustration at the tired old magazine. I attacked their junk sources of circulation, low-quality special sections, flimsy paper stock, behind-the-curve reporting, off-putting tone for women, and anything else I could find to attack. I dug deep and hit hard. I would show Mitch and the management team how it was done.

By 3:00 PM, I was laying it all into PowerPoint. All that remained was to drop in a separate second section that Lily and Matt were preparing for me: a dry market-share analysis to support an ad-prospecting discussion. I was sure I could breeze through that when the time came.

* * * *

JOHN AND I REVISITED the Del Frisco's bar before the Radio City event, but I nursed a single beer. I had learned that Mitch would be in attendance, so I was trying to behave myself. The last thing I needed was for him to see me stumbling around when he had just told me to stay focused. John blew off a bit more steam now that all the work he had put into Simon's forthcoming speech was finished.

After he settled the tab we strolled over to Radio City. The lobby was jammed with a Who's Who of big agency clients and Carlyle Nash higher-ups. Guests were four deep at the bar. John moaned.

"I hate these fucking things," he said. "I'd give my left nut to be at Donovan's."

He saw an opening in the bar crowd and snaked his way through to the front as I hung back. I surveyed the lobby to see if Mitch had arrived and spotted him a good 30 yards away in a group near the grand staircase. He was listening with rapt attention to the man in the middle of the circle: our aged chairman, Calvin Moreland. The company's eccentric patriarch was hard to miss. He was tall, reed thin, with a shock of tousled white hair, and, as always, he was rocking gently back and forth. Like Jack Benny, he held one hand across his chest and propped the other up under his chin—as if to prevent his head from falling forward. Mitch was just to his left, sporting what looked like a new basic blue suit and a fresh haircut. He typically dressed more stylishly for events like these, so I assumed he had arrived directly from a day of meetings. A woman excused herself from the circle and it cleared my view to the man to Calvin's right. He looked familiar—definitely a face I had seen in the building a time or two but also somewhere else. He was on the short side, thirtyish, with a nebbishy face.

As I searched my memory in vain, I noticed a woman carrying two drinks from the bar. It was Mary Ellen from our finance department, the woman whose beach ball I had stolen. She was back from maternity leave. I watched her work her way through the crowd and realized that she was heading for the chairman's circle. She handed one of the drinks to the nebbishy character and he put his free hand behind her back.

That's it! He's the guy in the wedding photo on her desk. What are they doing talking to Calvin Moreland?

John came back and handed me a beer. I pointed to the husband.

"Do you know who that guy is?"

John sipped his drink and looked over.

"Which one? The guy to Calvin's right?"

"Yeah. Who is he?"

"Oh, he's one of the dumb Morelands—Chase."

"He's a Moreland?"

"Yep. Hard to believe, I know. He looks like Mr. Potato Head."

"Mary Ellen is married to a Moreland?"

I heard someone shouting my name from about 15 feet away. It was Paige. She worked her way over. I introduced her to John.

"What are you doing here?" I asked.

"I'm a guest of Ramona Bloom from *Fine Estates*," she said impatiently. "I used to work for her. I need to talk to you."

John could tell that Paige wanted to talk privately so he tapped a nearby colleague and began chatting.

"I need to talk to you too," I said to Paige, "Did you know that Mary Ellen Tanner is married to a Moreland?"

"Of course I knew that. That's what I want to talk to you about."

"Why doesn't she have an office?" I asked.

"She was hired late, so they were all taken. That's why she has that special cubicle with the palace walls. Anyway, Mitch asked me if I had given her a beach ball while she was out. The mailroom said they did put one in her in-box, but I don't think I ever got it back. I think that's the one that's missing. Mitch thinks someone took it off her desk. He told me that if I don't find out what happened, it will be my problem. See? I told you. He hates me."

"Wait, wait, wait," I said, feigning ignorance. "I will never understand why this is so important to him."

Paige gestured to the Moreland circle.

"I think it's because he doesn't want the Morelands to know about it," she said. "With everything that's going on in the press, the last thing he needs is Mary Ellen finding out that someone was snooping around her cubicle. Even if it was only for a stupid beach ball. Lou Lamont eats this inside drama stuff up."

"This is ridiculous," I said.

"I know, but Mitch is getting so weird lately."

We were being called to our seats, so John looked over at me, pointed to his empty glass, and then to the bar. I nodded.

"Listen," I said to Paige, "Mitch wants to be CEO of this place someday. If he smells a crisis, big or small, he's going to do everything he can to snuff it out. I'll talk to you later."

As Paige strode away, I noted that I could make her problem go away as soon as tomorrow. I could bring in the beach ball and leave it on her desk with an anonymous note. *Found this behind a file cabinet in finance.* Or whatever. But I knew I wouldn't be doing that. The beach ball was—as John had called it—my severance, my leverage. But it was also something more than that. From the very first day I began working for him, Mitch had been in complete control of every facet of the operation. With Diane's departure, I was coming to realize that he had also been in effective control of every facet of my life. I'd given him that control, true. Diane was right about that. But still. Not anymore. I watched him as he and Calvin chatted privately on their way into the theater. He held the doddering old man's elbow as they walked slowly. I found myself hoping that Calvin was saying something along the lines of, "I'm not pleased, Mitch. You had better turn things around."

A simmering resentment stirred. The beach ball was staying right where it was: in my shitty little Hicksville apartment. *I* was in control now.

I walked back toward the emptying bar. John was ordering two last drinks.

"Here," he said. "It'll make the presentation bearable."

I quaffed two-thirds of the beer and ordered a shot of tequila.

"You want one?" I asked.

"No, I'm good. You OK?"

"I'm fine. But I think there's an outside chance the Morelands know about the beach ball. Or they will soon."

"Well, when you're worth thirty billion dollars, you make it your business to know everything. But I don't see why they would care. Do you think maybe you're overthinking—"

"I think they'd care for the simple reason that someone stole it off a family member's desk."

"Ah. That someone being you."

"And," I continued, "for the same reason Mitch wants it back. They don't need *World* and their golden boy future CEO taking another PR hit."

"Mitch isn't going to be CEO. Simon is in line for that. Maybe you should have another shot—"

"I don't know. Did you see Mitch hanging all over Calvin? While Simon is memorizing your speech backstage, Mitch is changing the chairman's diaper."

John shook his head.

"Never underestimate Simon," he said. "We should go in."

Our seats were in the second row of the orchestra section, a third of the way in. As we sidled past a few seated guests—colleagues of John—they cracked jokes about his lingering at the bar to the very last minute. In the far aisle seats of the third row sat Mitch and a client. Mitch was on the outside, leaning in and listening to his guest. As I made my way to my seat, he saw me. A fleeting look that said, "What's Paul doing here?" crossed his face, but he otherwise didn't acknowledge my nod. I took pleasure in the fact that my seat was closer to the stage than his.

As the lights dimmed, a recording of what sounded like a Bono song filled the theater. I didn't recognize the tune, so I figured Simon—a tireless cultivator of celebrity friendships—must have commissioned it for however many Moreland millions it took. I couldn't understand the lyrics all that well, but they seemed to be about emotion. The curtain rose and a film began, or I should say a music video began. Naked painted bodies writhed together. A drop of water fell from a red rose in close-up and landed on the cheek of a woman in a bathtub filled with petals. A lion cub was birthed, and a little boy carrying a sparkler ran through a field in slow motion. I had no idea what any of it had to do with magazines. I looked at John in wonderment.

"Were we supposed to get three-D glasses?" I whispered.

"You should have seen the first cut. There was footage of Gandhi in it. Simon loves this overwrought bullshit."

A freshly botoxed fashion editor turned and sneered at us. John mimed masturbation as she turned back to the screen.

The film eventually found its way to the main thrust of the advertising campaign: the emotional connection that readers allegedly have with Carlyle Nash magazines. Each brand was paired with a celebrity who presumably loved their title so much that they would have sex with each issue if they could. In the print ads, Gisele Bündchen curled up erotically with a copy of *Gloss*, George Stephanopoulos shared a hammock with a copy of *Bellwether*, and a post-workout Kobe Bryant sweated all over a copy of *True Gent*.

"Who are we targeting with this?" I asked John. "Readers or advertisers?"

"I don't know. Assholes of any stripe, I suppose."

Following a few intercut talking-head snippets of Carlyle Nash editors trying hard to sound like they cared about Carlyle Nash's reputation as much as their own, the film closed with a rapid montage of company logos set to ear-splitting techno funk music.

Rapturous applause erupted as Simon strode to the podium. Working from a printed copy of the speech, he opened with a joke about how indebted he was to the Morelands for financing a campaign costing more than the annual GDP of Peru. I checked to see if Calvin was laughing, but he just rocked back and forth, squinting up at the Carlyle Nash logo on the screen.

"Before I go on," said Simon, "I'd like to thank one of the most indispensable men in the business—my right hand, John Steffans."

As John stood up halfway and gave a quick wave, I thought it magnanimous of Simon to recognize his contributions so publicly. I also felt envious—or at least impatient for the day when my name might be spoken from the stage. I stole a glance back at Mitch and saw him busy with his Blackberry. My resentment began to stir again. I was certain he would never share credit with me or anyone for anything.

Simon was still looking down at John when his eyes shifted to me for a split-second.

Was that a wink? Did he just acknowledge me? Maybe I could work for this guy. Seems like he at least gives a damn about his people.

Mitch, on the other hand, didn't appear to need anyone but himself. I glanced back at him again. He kept working his Blackberry as Simon spoke, probably hounding poor Paige again or telling Calvin how much he liked his suit. I imagined myself climbing over the row, ripping the Blackberry out of his hands, and hurling it up into the mezzanine. Simon delivered a laugh line which I missed. The crowd roared.

John elbowed me.

"That was my best one," he said.

"Great stuff."

"Thanks. It's almost over," John added. "By the way, Simon wants to grab a drink with us after this."

"OK. Sounds good."

As I watched Simon control the big room with ease, I thought that maybe the time was finally right for me to make a move. John had always told me the door was open if I wanted to work with him. Perhaps it was now or never considering how *World* was taking its lumps. Maybe I should just roll the beach ball into Mitch's office and be on my way. But the nagging feeling that my work wasn't finished at *World* persisted—and the offsite would be a chance for me to shine once again.

My Blackberry vibrated. I opened the email.

Need to talk to you. See me after. —Mitch ▪

CHAPTER NINETEEN

Monday Late
(2007)

A S I WAITED at the bar following the event, I thumbed through a set of index cards I'd been carrying around since morning. Each referred to a slide in my *Globalist* presentation, and I was mentally rehearsing their corresponding click builds. For example, on a slide assailing the magazine's old white male tone, I had placed the cover of an issue featuring Warren Buffett on the left side of the screen and kept the right side blank. My plan was to say, "This issue contained photographs of more than sixty men and women. Do you know how many were men? Fifty-seven. And one of the three females was—*click*—Miss Piggy." And the photo that had accompanied an article on Muppets licensing would drop in. It was perfect. Miss Piggy's smiling face would fill the right half of the screen, and I would get the laughter I always craved when presenting. It had a way of both relaxing and fueling me.

I heard a woman to my left order a vodka gimlet, Diane's drink, so I turned to look. It was Mary Ellen. She knew me from the hallways, so she gave a polite wave. I waved back.

"Welcome back," I said.

She seemed slightly surprised that I knew she had been out on maternity leave: we'd never had much contact. She half-smiled.

"Thanks," she said.

She picked up her drink and raised a toast.

"Good to be out and about."

Her plump frame was squeezed into a red sequined designer dress. She looked like she was feeling the heat a bit as she took a gulp of her drink. A glittering bracelet strapped tightly around her meaty wrist looked like it had cost Chase Moreland five figures. I thought about the faux diamond-encrusted letter opener on her desk and wondered if the stones could possibly be real.

Damn, I should have stolen that thing too.

"Are you back into the swing of things yet?" I asked.

"Not yet. Today was my first day, but I spent most of it packing."

"Packing? Are you leaving us?"

"No, no. I'm just moving into an office. I need a little more privacy, so they're going to shift the floor plan around a bit."

"Oh...really?" I asked. "I haven't heard about that."

Chase approached her from behind. He was holding her handbag. He didn't acknowledge that she was talking to me.

"The car's waiting, dear," he whispered.

She stared straight ahead at the mirrored bar.

"I'm finishing my drink," she said.

Chase moved in closer. I pretended to study my cards and stopped breathing so I could hear him.

"Please make it just the one, Mary Ellen."

"Please leave me the fuck alone," she whispered.

"Mary Ellen, I think you're drunk."

"Oh shut up, Chase."

She guzzled the rest of her drink and snatched her bag from his hands. She turned to me.

"Nice talking to you," she said.

I glanced up. "You too," I said as she plodded away barefoot, holding her high heels. Chase placed a bill on the bar and scurried after her. I had had no idea she was such a formidable person. I picked up a cocktail napkin and began folding it into smaller and smaller squares.

Why was she moving into an office? Why now? It has to be connected in some way to the beach ball. Does she know it was stolen? Do the Morelands know? And where is she moving to? No one told me about a new floor plan. Why not? Wait a minute. Am I going to lose my office? Is that what Mitch is going to tell me? It makes some sense. If we swap with Finance, there will be one shitty little office for me and two cubes for Lily and Matt. And we'll be closer to Mitch's office too. Is he planning to keep a closer tab on me? Is that what's going on?

John wrapped up a conversation across the lobby and headed my way. Simon was talking to Calvin Moreland, whose driver was waiting patiently at the standard servant-to-the-filthy-rich distance. Mitch was near the exit talking to Paige, who was taking notes. I expected and wanted him to look for me when they finished—I was curious what he needed to talk to me about—but he waved goodbye to an acquaintance and walked out the door.

Shit. I guess he forgot. Or maybe it wasn't that important. Or maybe I am losing my office and he doesn't know how to tell me. Or... has he figured it out? Does he think I have the beach ball? Oh, for Christ's sake...stop fucking thinking. What's the matter with you?

"Thinking about the wife?" asked John.

"Huh? Oh...yeah. All day long."

"So what happened? You never told me."

I sighed.

"You know. Everything. This. The magazine. Fucking Mitch. But she's not perfect either..."

"You're sure it's not about Emily?"

"No. If she knew about that, she would have left me long ago. It's just that—"

"Fuck, wait," said John, "Here comes Simon. I'll talk to you about it later. Trust me, she'll come back after you come to work with me...asshole."

"I just might."

Simon approached with three brunettes in tow. The one pulling up the rear smiled broadly when she saw me. I only hazily recognized her face at first, but I knew who she was. It was Jennie. She winked and waved.

"Hi Captain!" she shouted.

Simon turned back to her.

"Oh, that's right," he said with a smile. "You two are already acquainted."

He shook my hand.

"Paul, so good to see you again."

"Hello Simon. It's good to see you too."

He put a hand on John's shoulder and gave an affectionate squeeze. Jennie, still smiling, circled to my right and stood next to me with her back to the bar. She was wearing a sunny floral print dress that didn't seem quite right for the occasion but fit her bubbly manner. She stood as close as an old friend, which made me wonder just how much I had shared with her on our drunken night of adventure. Simon turned to his other companions.

"Monica, Michele, please meet my new friend Paul."

"Nice to meet you both," I said.

Each woman was wearing a cocktail dress—one black, one royal blue—and they stood an inch or two taller than the rest of us.

"Monica," said Simon "is my creative services director and Michele is the best talent wrangler in media."

The bartender came around the bar with a tray of champagne glasses. Simon took one and handed it to me.

"And if you don't know about Paul, ladies, I have it on authority that the *World* launch wouldn't have broken my long-standing ad-page record without his brilliance."

"Not true," I said. "But thanks, Simon."

Jennie took a sip of her champagne.

"Helllloooo," she said. "This'll get my dress off."

"Paul?" said Simon.

"Excuse me?"

"Help the woman for God's sake."

They all laughed, and after a pause, I did too. But I couldn't stop thinking of what John had told me: that Simon and Jennie had a sexual relationship. It seemed completely at odds with his image as a man who could and perhaps did have regular sex with the statuesque women presently flanking him. And despite what Jennie had said about the champagne being good enough to get her dress off, I somehow knew she didn't mean it. Images of her laughing with me in Bryant Park started coming back, each consistent with the undeniable underlying wholesomeness I sensed in her. John had told me that nothing untoward had happened when I had gone out on the town with her that night, and that also made perfect sense. As she stood next to me beaming and guileless, I tried to remember more details from our scotch-soaked romp through Midtown. An image of her trying on a beret at the table of a street vendor came back. I looked at her and smiled. She winked back.

"So Paul," said Simon. "Tell me what you thought about the show."

I searched for the right adjective.

"Stunning," I said.

Simon nodded, but a slight squint of his eyes told me that he had caught the potential wiseacre ambiguity of my word choice.

"...and powerful," I added. "John told me to expect something special, but this exceeded my expectations. And I can't think of a better positioning for the company. It's perfect."

Simon smiled and nodded.

"Thank you, Paul. I do think every brand in the room was impressed. John, there are just a couple of script points I want to clean up, however..."

As John and Simon talked one-on-one, and Monica and Michele paired off too, Jennie elbowed me.

"How *are* you?" she asked.

"I'm great. Really great."

"How's the job?"

"It's fine. Big offsite coming up—"

"How's the baby?"

"He's awesome. Getting so big."

She shifted to a solemn tone.

"And how's your wife? You two still locking horns?"

My head spun. I shot a quick glance at John and Simon, but they were still locked in conversation.

"No, no," I said "Things are better now. We talked it out. How are you? What's going on with the... What's going on with you? Everything good?"

She placed her champagne flute on the bar and narrowed her eyes.

"I'm fine," she said. "So...did you end it?"

"Did I end it? Did I end what?"

She punched me in the chest.

"You didn't. What's the matter with men?"

"I'm sorry...Jennie. But I'm not sure what you're talking about."

She looked at the group to make sure no one was listening, then lowered her voice.

"The affair. Your mistress..."

I put my hand to my forehead.

"Jesus Christ. Is there anything I didn't talk to you about?"

She punched me in the chest again. Simon, in mid-sentence with John, noticed but didn't appear all that curious as to why.

"You don't remember," she said, "do you?"

"Not everything."

"So did you?"

"Did I what?"

"End it. The affair!"

"Not exactly. But... Why the hell am I talking to you about this? And don't punch me again."

Jennie sighed.

"We're talking about it because I thought we were friends."

"For God's sake. OK, yes, we're friends...I guess. I just... whatever. Yes, by the way, it is over. The affair. That's good, right?"

"Of course it's good. That's what I told you to do, dummy. You have a family."

"I do. I know. You're absolutely right. Thank you."

"Good boy, Captain. We can have some fun now."

"Are you gonna keep calling me Captain?"

"Yes," she said with a smile. "I like it. It fits."

Simon finished his champagne and looked around the emptying lobby.

"Why the hell are we still in this tomb?" he said. "To my car. Now. All of you."

We dutifully followed.

Calling it a car was an understatement, of course. As we climbed in, I noted to John that it was big enough to play field hockey in. Simon overheard.

"You're just brimming with ideas, Paul," he said. "We'll have to stop and get short uniforms for the ladies."

Monica and Michele rolled their eyes as if they knew this would only be the beginning of Simon's sexist comments.

"Nice going, Captain," whispered Jennie as we sat down on the limo's side couch, with John on her opposite side.

"That's not what I meant," I said.

"I know. Just don't set him up."

Simon settled in on the back couch, with Monica and Michele snug on each side. Monica's hand was already stroking his leg. If indeed Simon and Jennie were an item, I felt somewhat embarrassed for Jennie, but also self-conscious that she was treating me nearly like a partner. She had even looped her hand inside my arm as we had walked ahead of Simon from the bar to the limo. As John mixed gin and tonics for everyone, she noticed that the collar of my suit was sticking up. She gently leaned me forward and fixed it with both hands. I hoped

Simon wasn't watching; I didn't want him to think anything was going on. But as he seductively stroked Michele's arm, my feelings flipped to protectiveness toward Jennie. It was as if the quarterback who was dating my little sister was openly flirting with a pair of cheerleaders. John handed me a drink and I took a sip. Simon raised his glass in our direction, as John—looking like he'd had too many of these rides in the past—settled back in his seat.

"A toast," said Simon, "to an adorable new couple."

"We're friends, Simon," said Jennie. "He has a family. Do you remember those?"

Simon laughed.

"Sadly I do, dear. Pesky little things, aren't they, Paul?"

I looked at John for some hint that maybe he had already told Simon that Diane had left me. He read my mind and gave a quick headshake to indicate that he hadn't.

"Yep," I said. "If you see a woman in the Carlyle Nash building with dynamite strapped to her body, it's probably my wife."

"Really, mate? Over this ridiculous little company? Tell her it's not worth it. Come work with John and me, and I'll send the two of you to a conference in Paris. But you should just go with the flow like me. My third wife just left me because I couldn't stop sleeping with the first two. But she'll come around."

I wondered for a moment if either or both of the women hanging on him were former wives, but I didn't ask. John began bantering with Simon about marital politics, so I turned to Jennie. Given how transparent Simon was being about his sex life, I decided to cut to the chase.

"Can I ask you a personal question?"

"Sure. But I might not answer it."

"What's this about you having an affair with him?"

She sighed.

"An affair—as you are well and sadly aware, Captain—requires that one or both of the people participating is married to or living with someone else. So the answer is no."

"You know what I mean, Jennie."

"What I do with, Simon—what I *did* with Simon—is not something I'm proud of, but it happened. I'm not perfect."

"I didn't say you were. I'm not judging anyone."

"Sure you are. I can see it in your eyes. The difference is that I wasn't judging you when I asked you about your affair. Not that you remember. I just saw a nice person making a big mistake and I wanted to help."

People had been telling me I was a nice person for years, but it had been a long time since I'd felt like one. I took a sip of my drink.

"Well, I guess you did," I said. "It's over."

"But you didn't end it, did you? She did. Am I right?"

"What are you, psychic? I hate psychics."

She smiled.

"I just know people, Paul. I don't think you would have ended it."

"You called me Paul."

"Yeah," she said with a wink. "I like it. It fits."

I still wanted to ask her what I had specifically told her about the beach ball—and what she had told Simon—but the limo came to a stop. A now buzzing Simon led the charge out, arm in arm with Monica and Michele. John, drink still in hand, trudged just ahead of Jennie and me. He looked up.

"The Four fucking Seasons," he said, "I hate this place."

It was my first time back. As we entered and approached the bar, the memory of my initial rendezvous with Emily came back in Technicolor. I began to tell Jennie about it, but caught myself. It was better left unmentioned and in the past, even though a part of me wanted to hurtle back in time to the moment. In guilty reflex, my mind skipped to Diane and home. I wondered what she was doing, how she and Aidan were, what she had told her sister about us, if anyone had broken in to our presently unattended house, what my family was saying about me as they headed down to Philadelphia, if Uncle Frank was watching my every move. I imagined him sitting on the same bar stool that Emily had occupied.

Come here, you ungrateful little prick. Have a drink with your uncle.

I excused myself and headed to the men's room to splash cold water on my face and clear my head. After I dried off, I took inventory of my pockets: comb, lip balm, wallet, phone, and index cards. I sat down in a stall to flip through the cards for a minute. There was a particular slide transition that I liked but didn't love, so I began reciting it quietly.

"During a period in which the national audience of female professionals grew twelve percent, *The Globalist*'s market penetration dropped by..."

After a few more run-throughs, I made a timing adjustment in my head and committed it to memory. I realized that I had been in the stall for more than a few minutes, so I got up to return to the bar. As I walked back, I recalled the countless times I had done this to Diane at social events—losing myself in a single project point at the oddest moments. In our early years, she had treated it as a creative quirk she could live with. By the time Aidan came along, I could expect only a frustrated shake of her head upon my return.

Jennie's expression, on the other hand, was one of wonderment as to what had taken me so long. Simon, meanwhile, had the others laughing at a story—but he too looked up as I approached the bar. He pointed to my crotch.

"Christ, mate," he said. "You might want to save some of that for your new girlfriend here."

"Stop it, Simon," said Jennie.

I didn't have the energy to explain what I'd been doing in the stall, so I just shrugged and looked to see if John had ordered me a drink. A Heineken Light was waiting on the bar next to where Simon was standing in the middle of the group, sipping a martini. He saw me searching, picked up the beer, and gestured toward two empty stools further down the bar. I had been expecting this—the moment when he might finally corner me to learn more about the beach balls. Mitch knew how close I was to John, so I didn't want to reveal too much. If Simon started causing PR trouble for Mitch, it would be relatively easy for Mitch to connect the dots from Simon to John to me. However, I still didn't know specifically what I had already revealed to Jennie.

Simon noticed an empty side table and opted for it over the stools. He put down our drinks and pointed to one of the chairs with an open palm, inviting me to sit down first.

"I'm glad we're getting this chance to talk, Paul," he said. "My schedule is a bear for the next few days."

"I'm glad too. Although I'm curious what you want to discuss."

Simon chuckled as he undid his tie, pulled it off gently, and folded it. He called to Jennie.

"Jennifer, would you be a dear and hold this for me?"

Jennie, with an air of hating this part of her job, came over and took the tie. Her eyes met mine for an instant and I hoped I was conveying sympathy rather than judgment. She smiled professionally at Simon and took the tie.

"With pleasure," she said, "Your Highness."

"Thank you, love."

He took a sip of his martini and turned back to me.

"Come on now, mate. You know why we're here."

"OK. I do have some idea."

"Then let's not waste each other's time."

I was about to say, "OK, so you're curious about the beach balls," but Simon raised his hand just as I began to speak.

"For the past few years," he said, "whenever I've told John he should bring a strong second on board, he has said, 'Paul Cavanaugh would be perfect. I can get him.' But somehow he never does get you. Why not?"

Out of the corner of my eye, I saw John talking to Monica and Michele. Jennie was seated on a stool, and it was clear she was only pretending to care about their conversation. As I formulated an answer to Simon's question, I took in the wistful look on her face and knew in a flash that I had seen that expression at some point during our prior fun-filled night. If I could have, I would have gotten up to ask her if she was OK. I wondered why I cared so much, why I was piling even more concerns on my already bursting-at-the-seams life.

"It's hard to say," I replied. "It's just that...I guess the timing was always off. For example, when I was at *Bellwether*, we were so focused on profitability that I wanted to be a part of it. And working on the *World* launch kind of speaks for itself. I mean, who wouldn't want to—"

"Work for Mitch again?"

"Not really," I said unconvincingly. "It was about working for great brands."

Simon laughed again.

"Well," he said, "one out of two isn't all that bad, my friend. A time-tested magazine like *The Globalist* is a 'great brand.' *World* will be a mere footnote, I'm afraid."

"I think *World* can weather the bad press. As Mitch says, the category has a real opportunity, a white space for a magazine that can—"

"Yes, yes, the vaunted white space. Listen mate, that white space is turning into a black hole for this company."

A waiter dropped off a plate of appetizers. Simon picked up a piece of bruschetta and ate it in one bite.

"This goes no further," he continued. "The Moreland family is already a tad queasy about recessionary indicators for two-thousand-eight. And they're not terribly happy with the man who talked them into the flop of the decade."

"But it's not—"

"I know what you're going to say. It's not Mitch's fault that the editorial product was so poor. That's true. I lay that at the feet of Calvin Moreland himself for hiring that wet-behind-the-ears fool of an editor. What's his name?"

"Jimmy Stillman," I said.

"Yes, the boy. Anyhow, the fact remains that *World* Magazine will be the final big project for Mitch Blake at Carlyle Nash. After they shut it down—and they will shut it down—he'll be lucky to scramble back to *Bellwether.* But I suspect they'll park him at a lesser magazine until he's wise enough to take his ad-page record and move on."

I took a sip of my beer and reached for an appetizer. I didn't know what to say. Simon smiled.

"So then, Paul Cavanaugh, why in the world would you stay at *World?*"

I thought about the index cards in my pocket. As rough as the month had been, I still believed we could convince the ad community that *World* was a superior model for the category. I tried to separate Simon's dislike for Mitch from his seemingly logical and informed opinion that the magazine would eventually go under.

"I'm heading to a management offsite tomorrow," I said. "I think I'll come back with a much better idea of the magazine's outlook."

"So that's your way of telling me you'll be seeing things through to the end? If so, I may have to tell John that there are plenty of other strong seconds on the market."

Monica, Blackberry in hand, shouted from the bar.

"Simon! We won the Mazda business!"

"Splendid, darling." Simon said as he raised his glass. "I'll be there in a moment."

He turned back to me.

"Mazda. Not unexpected. An eighty-million-dollar account, Paul. Exclusive custom campaign across nine of our brands. Sadly though, *World* isn't on the media plan. You might think that was my doing, but it wasn't. It was Mazda's wishes. Their chief marketing officer called your magazine—and I quote—'a fucking mess.'"

I began peeling the label off my beer. I wondered when or

if he would inquire about the beach ball, but I wasn't going to bring it up first. He just sat there with a sly smile. I glanced over at John, who spread his arms out, palms upturned, as if to say, "What's it going to be, Paul?"

"Alright," I said. "Make me an offer."

Simon wiped the corner of his mouth with a napkin, smiled, and stood up.

"Excellent. You'll hear from us by next Monday." ▪

CHAPTER TWENTY

Tuesday - Wednesday
(2007)

P AIGE EMAILED ME the good news later that night
that Mitch wouldn't be in the office on Tuesday morning. He had personal business to attend to and would
be meeting us at Mohonk that evening. A luxury van
would be bringing me and the rest of the management team
north, but not until 3:00 PM.

So I slept in. That is, until Keith started tuning his motorcycle in the garage directly beneath my bedroom window. I
stretched out on my air mattress amidst the faint smells of
gasoline and stared up at the cracked ceiling that Diane used
to complain to Keith about. "Go ahead," he would always respond. "Paint it yourself. I don't care." But Diane would stub-
bornly insist that he was the landlord, so it was his job. *I should
call Diane*, I thought—like Jennie had told me to do the night
before.

Jennie and I had shared a car home from The Four Seasons at
roughly three that morning. Unlike our first semi-remembered
outing, I recalled every detail of the past evening. It turned out
that she was a Long Islander too, which perhaps explained our

natural connection. Throughout a trip that began with a traffic tie-up in the Midtown Tunnel and ended at the curb of her sister's house in Floral Park, where she rented a basement apartment, we had talked and talked. Two things she had said stuck with me: her advice that Simon would be just another version of Mitch, and her belief that nothing at Carlyle Nash was as important as friends and family. I knew she was right on both counts, but I still needed time to think about what I wanted to do. As I rolled off the air mattress, I envisioned her as I'd last seen her: bending down to pick up a *Pennysaver* in the moonlight and then disappearing around the side of her sister's house as the driver asked for my address.

She had also told me that the only thing she had shared with Simon about the beach balls was what I had originally shared with her: that Mitch had distributed them, then recalled them, and that one had gone missing and he was determined to get it back. Thankfully, neither she nor Simon knew that I was holding the missing one. She said that she had heard Simon laughing with someone on the phone about Mitch's beach-ball stunt the morning after our drunken evening, so she had mentioned what I had told her about the recall. As I started my shower, I wondered who had told Simon about the incentive in the first place and who he'd been talking to on the phone when Jennie had overheard him laughing. A Moreland perhaps? I had no way of knowing so I told myself not to obsess over it and to just focus on the task at hand: nailing my Wednesday presentation.

I brewed some coffee, sat down at the card table I had set up in the kitchen, and flipped through my index cards again. Not more than two cards in, I thought about Uncle Frank. I closed my eyes and imagined him in his open casket: grey hair slicked back, a peaceful half-smile on his face beneath his ruddy nose. When I opened my eyes, I saw him seated across the card table. He was blowing smoke rings—just as he used to do in my parents' house, sitting on their 1970s-era plastic-covered couch.

The vision was vivid enough that I wanted to poke my finger into the middle of the rings as they drifted just past my face and over my shoulder.

"Uncle Frank. Can you do that—"

I heard a thump against my kitchen window and turned to see what it was. A few seconds later, what looked like a Nerf football hit the window square in the middle again. I crossed to the window and opened it. Keith was standing in the yard holding a brown paper bag.

"Hey," he said, "the deli delivered the wrong fucking bag again. There are like four egg sandwiches in here. You want one?"

"Yeah, sure. Thanks. I'll be down in a minute."

I threw on a casual work outfit, grabbed an overnight bag packed with a change of clothes, and headed downstairs. Keith was kneeling in front of his motorcycle when I arrived in the garage. He worked a socket wrench with his left hand and his sandwich with his still-bandaged right. Egg yolk dripped down both his grease-stained wrist and his trucker moustache. I reached into the brown bag on his workbench and pulled out a sandwich marked "BEC" in black marker—bacon, egg, and cheese.

"By the way," I said. "I won't be home tonight. I have a business trip upstate."

"What am I, your mother? I don't give a shit. Come and go as you please."

"I know that, Keith. I'm just trying to be courteous."

"I get it," he laughed. "She left you because you're a homo, right?"

"Yeah. I am. He's moving in tomorrow."

"If his checks clear, I got no problem."

He washed down his sandwich with a Red Bull and stood up.

"What's upstate?" he asked.

"My boss is taking me and a few other people to a strategy meeting at the Mohonk Mountain House."

"You're going upstate to have a meeting? Don't you have a conference room in your building?"

"It's an offsite. It's hard to explain."

I paused to take a bite of my sandwich.

"Actually," I continued, "it's not hard to explain. It's incredibly stupid. We're traveling to a remote hotel to use their conference room instead of ours. My company excels at wasting money."

Keith shook his head.

"You can have your meeting in my fucking basement," he said. "I could use the money more than the Mohunk Mountain House."

"Mohonk," I corrected.

"Whatever. But seriously, if your company ever needs air-conditioning work, call me. I'm broke, dude."

"I think they've got that covered, Keith. But if I hear of anything…"

I glanced at my watch and realized that the next train out of Hicksville was leaving in 20 minutes. Keith started his motorcycle and went back to work on it.

"Thanks for breakfast," I shouted.

He gave a wave of his socket wrench.

* * * *

PAIGE HAD PROMISED she would save me a seat next to her on the van, but I was last to board and, by then, Jonah Wilen, who headed up *World.com*, had taken the spot. Six other members of the team were paired off too. Just one open seat remained: next to Thad.

"Nice of you to join us," he said as he moved his Coach tote bag off the seat to make room for me.

He had a Band-Aid over his right eyebrow from his accident at the Bloomingdale's White Sale.

"Some of us have work to do, Thad. Right up to the last minute."

He waved his Blackberry at me.

"Some of us know how to manage our time," he said.

I threw my bag up on the luggage rack and offered to put his up too. He clutched it to his chest, as if my hands were covered in grease.

"I'll need access to it," he said.

I sat down.

"No problem. I wouldn't want you to be getting up and down for your hand cream for two hours."

"Exactly," he said. "The horror."

As the van pulled out into traffic, we read and responded to emails in silence for several minutes. I noticed that Thad had sent me one the night before, inquiring if I could take care of a data request from a client. I knew the numbers off the top of my head, so I emailed them directly to the contact we both knew. I elbowed Thad and showed him his original email.

"I took care of this," I said.

"Would you please email me that?"

"Email you what? It's your email."

"Just email me that you took care of it."

"No, Thad. I just told you in person. Why should I email you too?"

He turned and stared at me.

"There needs to be a written record of things, Paul. It's professional."

"OK, Thad. Fine."

Brimming with the confidence of a man being pursued by Simon Bell, I typed the words *Bite me* and thrust the Blackberry in Thad's face.

"How's that?" I said. "Does that work?"

I expected him to react angrily, but he smiled.

"I want that. Hit *send*...please. I'll forward it to HR."

I typed *Took care of this* over my first message and sent it.

"Bite me," I said.

"Sorry, Paul. I'm busy tonight."

I took out my index cards.

"So," he said, "We'll finally get to see your *Globalist* deck. You've had enough time. It better be good."

"Oh, it's good. I'm gonna rip them a new asshole."

"Charming," he said as he took a pair of Bose headphones out of his bag and put them on.

My Blackberry vibrated in my hand. The email, with an empty subject line, was from Diane: *I spoke to your Mother. Where are you? Why didn't you go to your Uncle's funeral?*

I replied immediately: *I couldn't bear to go. I swear it had nothing to do with work. Obviously I'm depressed and I miss you and Aidan. You won't believe this: I'm staying at Keith's. Our old apartment was empty. It will do for now. You can take Aidan home. I want to talk to you.*

Her response: *I just wanted to make sure you were OK. Amazing about apartment. Thanks. Aidan will be happier at home. I will call you when I am ready. It may not be soon. I still have a lot to think about.*

I responded with *OK, Diane. I understand. XO.* I watched and waited for the next few minutes, but instead of a response, a message from Jennie arrived: *Enjoyed our talk last night. Good luck upstate. See you soon.*

For the next 90 minutes, the ride was quiet. As we pulled into Mohonk, Thad announced that Mitch would now *not* be meeting us for dinner. Whatever business he'd been attending to had kept him in Manhattan, so he wouldn't be arriving until morning. As fine as I was with that, I was surprised at just how often his schedule was changing unexpectedly of late. Traditionally, if Mitch said he would be at Point A at Hour X, you could set your watch by it. Questions abounded.

Is he being grilled by the Morelands? Did one of his kids get hurt again? Is he having an affair? Would he have an affair? Should I call Emily to see how she's doing? Is the Irish journalist just a fling? Will my room have a minibar? Stop it, you idiot. Stay sharp for the presentation. Read a book and go to bed. Or just one drink and done. No, take a bath. Do some sit-ups. Jerk off.

* * * *

JENNIE HAD SAID that God's work is all around us, if only we'd look. Judging by the fact that my room had no minibar and no television, I thought that she might be on to something. Clearly, someone upstairs wanted me to lie down and get some rest—maybe even that old partier himself, Uncle Frank. But an espresso after a light dinner had me wired, so I read the most recent issue of *Bellwether* from cover to cover. I saw that Emily had taken a break from the war zone to pen a piece about genetically engineered food. It held my interest, but not nearly as much as when she wrote about almost being blown up by a roadside bomb. Not that I was bitter.

I drifted off to an image of my father sitting in the rocking chair in my room, reading the *Tribune*. He and my mother had once stayed at Mohonk, but they had both found it more boring than relaxing. It was indeed the quietest hotel I'd ever stayed in. I pictured my father nodding off the way he always did at Saturday evening mass when I was a boy. I'd nudge his forearm when it was time to stand up for the Gospel and watch him shake off the exhaustion of another 50-hour week.

I woke the next morning semi-refreshed and wondered if Mitch had arrived yet. Sure enough, he had sent a group email at 3:00 AM saying that breakfast would still be at 7:30, but the agenda would begin a little earlier than planned—at 8 instead of 8:15. There was much to cover, he wrote, and every minute counted. Paige slid a revised agenda under everyone's door before breakfast. My 10:00 AM time slot remained the same. I shaved and showered while rehearsing my slide builds. Just as I finished dressing, there was a tap on the door. I let Paige in and she sat down on the edge of the queen bed.

"I thought I might need to wake you up," she said.

"Had there been a minibar, maybe. I don't know why anyone

would stay at this place on their own. It's like a monastery."

"Mitch likes it. He thinks it will make for a focused day. If so, it will be the first focused day of my year."

"Everything OK?"

"I think so. I spoke to him a few minutes ago and he seems happy with the prep. And he didn't say anything about that stupid beach ball for once. I guess he's finally stopped caring or he's figured out who took it. Dumbest thing ever."

As alarmed as I was by the latter possibility, I was nearly as concerned with the former. I didn't want Mitch to stop caring. I wanted to see him counting and recounting the beach balls into old age, forever coming up one short and wondering who was keeping it from him. Like Citizen Kane and "Rosebud," I imagined him on his deathbed, weakly whispering "Beach ball, beach ball," surrounded by puzzled nurses.

As we headed downstairs, I considered the possibility that Mitch did in fact know I was the culprit. I entered the dining room with some apprehension. My palms broke into a cold sweat.

Mitch was already seated at the head of a banquet table large enough for the entire team. A half-eaten cream cheese bagel sat to his left as he made notes on a steno pad. He didn't look up at anyone as we filtered in, loaded our plates with carbs, and sat down amidst small talk.

Paige announced to those of us giving presentations that everyone would get bound printouts of the PowerPoint files we had sent her. I hadn't known this was the plan, and I didn't want anyone reading ahead as I clicked through, so I hoped I could convince her not to hand my decks out until afterward. As I gulped down my first cup of coffee, I realized that I had never asked Paige about the audiovisual setup. I had simply assumed there would be a standard projection screen at the head of the table in the conference room. It was unlike me not to ask, and I chided myself for not checking.

Fuck. Come on, come on.

Paige was locked in conversation with Thad, so I went to check the room myself. It was down the hallway, just past the hotel's communal television room—which looked like it was there just in case a televised national tragedy took place. Not that such an event would interrupt our schedule. Rumor had it that on 9/11, Mitch had called a meeting at *Fine Estates* to discuss how the event might impact the magazine's airline advertising. If I had to guess, he had probably started that day with the same focused look I had just seen at breakfast. My stomach began to churn a bit as I entered the sunlit wood-paneled conference room.

Behind what would be Mitch's seat at the head of the table was a wide window overlooking Lake Mohonk. It was a beautiful view, but what I wanted to see was a wall and video screen, not a mountain-ringed lake. I turned to the young hotel worker who was filling water glasses at each seat. He looked back and said "Good Morning" in a thick Scottish accent.

"Same to you," I replied. "Would you by any chance know if they'll be moving an audiovisual setup in here for our meeting?"

"I don't believe so, sir. But I'll be glad to find out for you."

"Thanks, but that's OK. I'm heading back to breakfast. I'll find out there."

He offered again, but I had already left to track down Paige. She was heading my way, carrying a stack of printouts.

"Shit, Paige. Isn't there going to be an AV setup?"

"No, Paul. I told you already. Mitch said we would just present around the table with printouts. He didn't want to get bogged down with tech and videos."

"You never told me that, Paige!"

"I sent an email on Friday! Trust me, Paul. You were on it. You must have missed it. You were probably..."

She trailed off as she entered the conference room.

I followed her in.

"I was probably what, Paige?" I asked as she went around the table, distributing printouts. She didn't answer, but I knew what she meant. I had probably been drunk.

"Fuck off, Paige." I said.

She spun around.

"Paul!"

She looked wounded and exhausted.

"I'm so sorry, Paige. I shouldn't have said that. I'm just stressed out."

"It's OK," she said quietly. "Listen, it'll be alright. I have all your printouts here. You'll do fine."

"I don't know," I said, "I thought I would be clicking through it. I have all these builds and transitions, and there's a video clip at the beginning."

"Don't worry. Just make the points you need to make."

"I'll try. Listen, I'm sorry again for what I said. And you were probably right too."

"Forget it."

I sat down at my assigned seat—two chairs down the table to Mitch's right, with Paige between us—and picked up a copy of my presentation. As colleagues began shuffling in, I knew I would have virtually no time to adjust. Thad and Jonah took their seats across from me, while the rest of the team settled in on both sides of the table to my right. Just seconds later, Mitch entered. He moved his water glass to a side table, turned off his phone, spread out his materials neatly, and underlined a heading at the top of his pad.

"OK," he said, "let's get started."

For the next 90 minutes, we reviewed an exhaustive status list of every client who had advertised in our launch issue. Mitch admitted that the attrition rate was certainly higher than expected, but he maintained that when the media noise around *World* died down after the fourth-quarter issues, we would have a viable long-term franchise. In his analysis, there would be enough advertising to go around for our magazine, *Currents*, and *The Globalist*.

"Let's grow the pie," he summed up. "It can be done. Continue to stress the value of the elite new readers we'll be bringing to the category, and good things will happen."

My heart began to beat faster as I realized that this message somewhat undercut the thrust of the presentation I was minutes from giving: that *The Globalist* could and should be destroyed. Mine was a pure, no-holds-barred, negative sell. I had to think of a way to ease into it softly, but the break before I went on would be just eight minutes long. Everyone else scrambled up to go to the restroom or check email, but I just sat there and closed my eyes for a minute. When I opened them, I saw Uncle Frank again. He was sitting on a high stool just behind the opposite right corner of the table. Tim Calhoun, our head of merchandising, came back into the room and sat down at the corner chair—but the vision persisted. My uncle sat perched about eight feet behind Tim, like a chair umpire. He was drinking what looked like a bottle of beer from the sixties: squat and brown, probably a Piels or a Schmidt's. He was smoking a Lucky Strike. He winked at me, took a long drag, and blew a smoke ring straight up in the air. I watched it ascend, just like I did as a kid, before it dissipated a few inches below the ceiling. I closed my eyes again and rubbed my temples.

"You good?" asked Tim.

"Yeah," I said, a bit startled. "No choice now."

"You're always solid. No worries."

"Thanks Tim."

The rest of the team returned, with Mitch and Thad last to their seats. They whispered as they sat down, and I wondered what they were saying.

They've already read my deck. They think it's off point. Or maybe Mitch... Shit. He's going to ambush me about the beach ball. Wait. No. Would he?

My mouth felt dry and my throat tightened. I reached for my water and took a sip. My hand shook slightly as I placed the glass back on the table. Thad smiled broadly and clapped his hands for attention.

"OK, everyone," he said. "It's time for Paul. The always entertaining Paul."

I knew exactly what he was doing: raising the bar high. I could tell by his fake smile that he wanted me to fail. I shot a glance at Uncle Frank, who made a limp-wrist gesture and mouthed the words "Fuck him" to me. He pulled a pop-top off a can of Schaefer and tossed it to the floor. The beer foamed over his hand and dripped down, but he patted the can dry with his cigarette hand.

"So," I said, "everyone has a copy?"

They were all staring down at page one. Mitch was already scribbling notes on his. I had planned on starting with a joke about the relationship between mountain air and market share, but I knew it wouldn't work.

"Here we go. Well…for starters…um, that big black box you see on the opening slide was supposed to be a video. I know…I missed the email about this being an over-the-table session. Very sorry about that. Anyway, I'll need to describe the video because it sets up the next slide."

Jonah paged ahead.

"*Wait!*" I said, "Please don't page ahead."

Uncle Frank laughed.

"Smooth, kid," he said. "Way to control the room."

"I'm sorry," I said to Jonah. "There's kind of a payoff after the video."

"The video you'll be *telling* us about?" he asked.

I badly wanted to ask him why he was wearing a blue blazer over a white t-shirt bearing a Green Hornet logo but I stopped myself. Mitch, looking impatient, took out his Blackberry and set it on the table.

"Yes," I said as I turned toward the colleagues to my right. "The video was, is, of Wilford Evans. The guy has been running *The Globalist* for so long that he's lost touch completely."

My voice cracked on the last phrase, so I gulped down some water. After I set down my glass, Paige refilled it from a pitcher. The sound of the cascading ice hitting the bottom of a glass made me turn toward Uncle Frank, but he was staring at the ceiling and blowing smoke rings again. Tim noticed I was gazing at a point just above his head and turned and looked behind him. I turned back toward Mitch and saw him staring at me. We made eye contact. His hands were folded in front of him.

"You were saying..." he said.

"Yes, sorry. So...the Evans video. He was at a conference in Aspen and he was talking about how great his magazine is and how bad he thinks ours is. Then he said, '*The Globalist* is written by young, hard-charging guys who kick ass all day.' He sounded ridiculous. Now if you go to the next slide..."

Thad raised his hand but didn't wait for me to call on him.

"When was the conference?" he asked.

"I don't know. About a week ago."

He glanced at Mitch and then spoke in his general direction.

"Oh, OK. I just thought a video of our main competitor might have been something you would have shared with us immediately."

Mitch took Thad's cue.

"Yes," he said. "Why didn't you email that around, Paul? You know it's important that we stay on top of industry chatter. We may not have responded to his needling, but I do want to know what's being said about us... right away."

"I'm sorry Mitch. It's just that I wanted to use it today, but then you—I mean we—decided to not have AV, and then—"

"Fine, fine." he said as he looked at his watch, "Let's move on. What are the main points here? I don't want to fall behind."

Uncle Frank stirred.

"I think your boss needs to get laid," he said.

I turned toward his corner.

"Stop it," I whispered.

Tim looked puzzled.

"Stop what?" he asked. "I didn't say anything."

"Sorry. Not you, Tim. I mean…it's nothing. Sorry."

I took another sip of water. Jonah stared at me curiously from across the table. Thad looked delighted. Paige squeezed my left thigh under the table. She then positioned my presentation copy in front of me. She had moved a few slides ahead to a more straightforward discussion of *The Globalist*'s declining circulation.

"Is this the slide you want to move to, Paul?" she asked in a motherly tone. "It looks interesting."

I could feel sweat trickling down my lower back. But as logical as it would have been to just leap ahead in the presentation and get it over with, I became determined to score the opening payoff.

"No," I nearly shouted.

I grabbed the deck and tried to shuffle back to the front, but the tightly ringed binding was giving me a problem. I grabbed an end of the black wire and ripped it violently away from the pages.

"Please, everyone, bear with me and go back to the slide after the video. This one."

I held up a slide with eight headshot photos of older-looking men on it.

"You see," I said breathlessly, "this would have followed the comment by Evans about young ass-kickers. The fact is that their entire stable of columnists is ancient. That's the joke, basically. I know, I know… If you have to explain a joke, then the joke—well, whatever. But then I had a couple of fun back-pocket facts too. You see this guy? Hamilton Hart? Three DWIs. I found that on Lexis-Nexis. You wouldn't believe the shit you can unearth there. Thom Canty? Filed for bankruptcy twice and now there's a lien on his house. He's their fucking financial columnist. William Howell? His daughter did time for prostitution and pill-pushing."

I hadn't really planned on using any of the personal dirt beyond the crack about a bankrupt financial writer. Most of it was material for post-meeting drinks. But I couldn't put the cork back in the bottle now. I picked up my water and guzzled it. I wished I were drinking something harder.

"And Wilford Evans himself..." I added. "He flies off to fuck boys in Haiti. Every Christmas break. But you've probably heard that one."

I leaned forward to air out my sweaty back. A few drops of urine escaped into my underwear. The room was deathly silent. I watched Uncle Frank get off his stool and walk to the window behind Mitch. He looked out at the lake. His shoulders shook like he was stifling laughter. Then Thad held up a slide.

"Thanks for that, Paul," he said. "Me? I'd like to know what Miss Piggy is doing in your presentation."

Mitch put his hand up. He spoke with controlled anger.

"Enough," he said. "Paul, I know you put a fair amount of work into this project, but I've paged ahead and I don't see it as something we'd necessarily lead in the market with. Unless, that is, pill-pushing prostitutes and the magazines that indirectly support them somehow becomes a topic of debate in the industry. I personally don't believe it will. I'd tell you to take a break and get some fresh air, but everyone's time here is valuable. So we're going to move ahead to the second half of your deck, the market-share analysis, and hope we get something out of it. Please go to slide number twenty, the pharmaceutical category, and take us through it—joke free please."

I sat up straight in my chair and exhaled. I took another sip of water.

"Can I go to the bathroom first?"

Mitch looked down and shook his head in frustration.

"Forget it," I said. "It can wait. Let's do this."

I gathered the *Globalist* portion of my deck and dropped the slides at my feet. I leafed to the section that had been prepared for me by Lily and Matt.

"Pharma," I said. "Big pharma...very big Pharma."

Paige laughed nervously. Mitch and Thad each shot her a cold look.

"Well," I plodded on, "if you look at the pie chart, you'll see that lead market share in our wider category is held by *Currents*. They have a pretty big lead on...Wait, sorry, it's actually pretty close there. Got my wedges mixed up. I thought the red wedge was...whatever. So, um, *The Globalist* is right behind. Then in the info box at right, you'll see that the biggest spenders in the category are Pfizer, Merck—"

My voice began to crack again. I wasn't sure if I was technically breathing. Mitch gripped his Blackberry with clenched hands.

"Paul," he said. "I think we can all read. Why don't you share with us some intelligence that's not on the page? Where is the category headed? Who'll be spending more next year? Who might cut budgets? Any big products coming off patent? What about over-the-counter drugs? Where are the opportunities?"

I looked down at the loose sheets in front of me and began rifling through them. I felt like I was back in the fifth grade and Mrs. Kliger was telling me that while my book report was well written, I should be able to explain why Harry S. Truman was called "that haberdasher from Kansas City." *What is a haberdasher, Paul? Why didn't you look it up in your dictionary? Short cuts won't do when you get to junior high, Paul.*

I reached for my water glass, but it was empty. I went back to shuffling the papers.

"I think," I said, "I have a section here that talks about opportunities, but I know there's, um, Pfizer and, uh, Olufsen."

"Olufsen?" said Thad. "Are they new?"

"Yeah. I think that, um."

Mitch was seething. I looked over at him with a pleading expression. *Please let me stop. Just take over the discussion.*

He scribbled a note and seemed to calm himself. I waited. He looked up.

"Move to consumer electronics, Paul."

I bowed my head, closed my eyes, and put my hands to my temples. After ten or so seconds of pained silence, I placed my palms atop my blurry mass of charts and I pushed the papers toward the center of the table.

"I can't," I said. "I'm having a bad day."

My meltdown was over...or had perhaps just begun.

I slid slowly back into a slumped position, my head against the back of my chair. Beneath my feet, I felt the papers I'd dropped to the floor.

"Jonah," said Mitch, "let's switch gears to online. How is pharma looking for *World.com* and our competitive sites?"

Jonah looked over at me with a combination of disbelief and compassion. But then he soldiered on, displaying what sounded vaguely like a firm grasp on the topic. I sat there numbly for at least three minutes as words and phrases like "merger," "sector growth," "robust," and "share point" volleyed back and forth over me.

I looked toward the window. Uncle Frank was still there. His shoulders were still shaking. But I realized now that he wasn't laughing. He turned and looked at me with tears in his eyes. He lit another cigarette and took a long drag. No smoke rings this time.

"They're lowering my ass into the ground right now, kid," he said. "But I'm glad this went so well for you."

And then he was gone. And then I began to cry too. Not just with misty eyes and sniffles, but with a great heaving sob followed by body-shaking wails. I pushed myself away from the table and stumbled out. Paige followed hard on my heels, took my arm, and led me down the hall past hotel reception, and out into the sunlight. I sat down on a curb. She sat next to me and put her arms around me. I felt pathetic and broken.

"Can you call me a car?" I asked.

"I will," she said. "Let's just sit for now." ·

CHAPTER TWENTY-ONE

Wednesday Late
(2007)

A S THE CAR PULLED OUT of Mohonk, the driver began to make small talk. I mumbled a polite response to his comment about how beautiful it is upstate when the trees begin to change colors. But for all I cared at that moment, they could have razed the forests and built strip clubs and rib joints. *Who gives a fuck? Live, work, crash, burn, die.*

As he switched gears to college football, I semiseriously thought about opening my door and rolling out into the center lane. I wondered how it would feel to have gravel embedded in every inch of my flesh, and if I would be able to scramble to my feet before a big rig took me out. I imagined that the impact wouldn't even hurt. There might even be a momentary rush as I hurtled through the air—like when T.J. O'Donnell tackled me over the middle in a pick-up football game when I was 15. The driver kept chattering as I replayed the tackle over and over. I had leapt high to make the catch at virtually the same time T.J. came at me like a guided missile. When I hit the turf, I marveled that I had held on to the ball. I wasn't the best athlete among my brothers, and I remembered wishing that Dad could have seen the play—but he had been called into the office that Saturday on a critical project. Later that evening, I had gone to my parents' room to tell him about it and found him sitting on the edge of the bed, holding his head in his hands and muttering about "this damn job, it just never lets up," as my mother rubbed his back. I thought of Diane. I needed to talk to her.

Paige had sat with me on the curb for a good 40 minutes after my meltdown and let me talk. I had told her everything that was going on in my personal life: about Diane's departure, and my current place of residence, and finally about my uncle's death. When I told her I had skipped his funeral for the meeting, her jaw had dropped.

"Oh, Paul," she had said. "You're kidding me. You know, Mitch isn't a monster. He would have understood."

"Really Paige? Did you see him in there? He wanted to destroy me for ruining his special fucking offsite. Among whatever other reasons he had."

The possible "other reasons" were key. I couldn't get past the nagging suspicion that he had indeed figured out that I had the beach ball. Paige had said that he had finally stopped hounding her to track it down. Why? Perhaps because he had solved the mystery on his own. While it was true that my performance at the conference table was cause enough for him to grill me as mercilessly as he had, the malevolent look in his eyes told me that there was more to it than that. When he had said 'Move to consumer electronics, Paul' I had felt certain: I was in Mitch Blake's crosshairs. It almost didn't matter why. Staring out the car window, I decided it was time to ruin him. Kill or be killed.

The truth was that I hadn't unloaded on Paige about my crumbling personal life just to gain her sympathy. I had also had an ulterior motive: swift damage control. Simon and John were formulating an offer to me at that very moment, so it was critical that as the story of my meltdown spread, it be accompanied by qualifiers like "death in the family," "estranged wife," "kicked out of his home," and "misses his kid"—not to mention "a gross miscommunication on audiovisual needs that pushed a strong, content-jammed presentation off the rails."

My personal PR spin on events needed to be: *Sure, Paul Cavanaugh lost it a bit upstate, but the poor guy was dealing with a perfect storm of shit at the time. Anyone else would have been a no-show at an offsite under those circumstances. But not Paul.*

Paige had unwittingly gotten the PR-spinning started even before I left. As I had sat on the curb waiting for my car, she had gone back inside to get my overnight bag and briefcase... and update the others. Almost immediately, different members of the team had started coming out for a minute to pat me on the back and say something along the lines of "Damn, Paul, you should have given yourself a break with all that stuff going on at home. Take it easy. You'll get through this." Tim had come out first, then Jonah, then—to my surprise—Thad.

"Welcome to my Sunday night phone calls with Mitch," he said, sitting down next to me on the curb. "That you never had to face that before speaks volumes about your work, Paul."

He paused.

"...And I'm sorry about stirring the pot in there."

I had started crying again as I shook his hand. Who would have thought it? I was bonding with Thad.

Mitch, on the other hand, had never come out.

The driver took a static-filled call from his dispatcher. As the car zoomed down the Palisades Parkway, one thought filled my mind: vengeance. I took out my Blackberry and logged into the SavageMktr9@hotmail.com account for the first time since Emily had ended the affair. I opened a new message and in the *TO* line I entered an address I had memorized days earlier: Lou_Lamont@nytribune.com.

* * * *

I TOLD THE DRIVER to take me to the Bryant Park Grill instead of home to the apartment. I had emailed John to meet me for a drink because I wanted to get out in front of the story. He was at the bar when I walked in. He knew, of course, that my personal life was rocky, so after I gave him a quick summary of my performance at Mohonk, he said not to worry about it. He smiled and said that he himself had once tried to strangle a boss in his earlier days.

"You're shitting me."

"Nope. I had already quit because he was a complete asshole. He tried to get back at me by refusing to sign my last expense report."

"You really strangled him?"

"I tried. We just rolled around on the floor until neither of us could breathe. It was pathetic. But worth it."

As for Simon, John said never to mention Delta Airlines to him—because he had once locked himself in a bathroom during a Delta flight to L.A. to berate his own reflection.

"For ninety minutes. The plane had to land in Dayton."

"Yeah, but what do I say if he asks about Mohonk?"

John chuckled. "Tell him you believe in making a grand exit. Really, I wouldn't worry about it. If anything, he'll probably tell you it's a sign that it's definitely time for you to leave *World*."

John was meeting his son for dinner, so he couldn't stay.

"Are you going to be OK?" he asked.

I nodded.

"You should call Jennie if you want company."

I wasn't sure I did, but he dialed her number before I knew what he was doing.

"Here," he said, handing me his phone.

"No. Wait. I don't know if I—"

But she had already picked up.

"Simon Bell's office. Jennie speaking... Hello? Hello?"

"Jennie," I said. "It's Paul."

"Paul! How are you? How was the meeting?"

"It was awful, but I'll tell you about it later."

"Are you still there?"

"No, I'm actually at the Bryant Park Grill with John. Do you want to come over?"

She paused. I figured she was distracted by work.

"Bryant Park Grill," she said flatly. "Do you ever go to the movies, Paul?"

"The movies. It's been a while."

"Meet me at the AMC on West Forty-Second in ten minutes," she said.

I had set out to get drunk, but the movies sounded like an oasis.

"OK, I'll be there."

"Great. And ten minutes is not enough time to order another drink."

She hung up. I handed the phone back to John.

"Looks like I'm going to the movies."

"See *Knocked Up*," he said. "It's pretty funny."

"Whatever she wants."

John finished his vodka cranberry, got up, and took his jacket from the back of his stool.

"That's the kind of attitude that makes second marriages work," he said with a smile.

"It's not like that. Really."

"I'll talk to you tomorrow," he said, throwing a $20 on the bar.

I handed it back to him.

"Let me get this. I owe you. A lot."

He put it in his pocket and patted me on the back.

"Don't worry about today," he said. "Doesn't change a thing. Fuck Mitch. Call in sick tomorrow. Sleep in."

"I might. Thanks John."

I paid the tab as he left. He had ordered a water on the side but hadn't drunk it. As I looked at it, I thought back to the sound of ice falling into my glass when Paige had refilled it at the offsite. I mourned my presentation's slide builds and the back-pocket one-liners I'd never get to share. I searched down the bar for Uncle Frank, but I didn't see him. At the far end sat a Wall Street type. He was reading *The Globalist...* of course. I turned to look at the tables behind the bar filled with Midtown workers de-stressing. Uncle Frank wasn't there, either. But out beyond the windows, on a bench in the park, sat my father— soaking in the early evening sun. He looked exactly as he did in my favorite photo of him: happy and relaxed at the start of what would be two short years of post-retirement living—actually just 21 months. He smiled as a pair of street musicians carrying horns walked by. After they passed, he was gone. I turned back to the bar and drank John's water.

* * * *

THE THEATER WAS JUST DOWN 42ND, so I beat Jennie there. I waited in the lobby next to a ticket machine; she arrived out front a moment later. I watched as a couple with a map in their hands, clearly tourists, asked her for directions. She happily stopped to help them as I walked outside to meet her. She was wearing another bright floral dress and flats. I tapped her on the shoulder and she turned.

"Hey!" she said, kissing me on the cheek.

"Hi, Jennie."

"You look tired."

"You like nice," I said, gesturing to her outfit. "I really like the way you dress."

"Thanks, Paul. It's nice to hear that..."

She led me into the theater.

"Believe me, my look isn't so popular with the building's black-clad stiletto crowd, but I don't care. I wear what makes me happy."

"Good for you."

She smiled.

"I'm glad you called," she said. "We probably both need this. And you know what? Simon wanted me to go out with him tonight. But I chose you. I'm not making that mistake again."

"Good for you again."

We did opt for *Knocked Up*, and I sprung for the tickets. She bought me Raisinets and pretzel nuggets and joked that it might mean having to miss a payment on her college loan. The movie was just starting when we sat down. She whispered to me that she wanted to hear all about my presentation afterwards.

"You may find it funnier than the film," I whispered back.

I laughed out loud throughout the movie, but at times, the laughter was the kind that's so close to crying that your body is simply seizing the opportunity to release pent-up emotion, stored madness. Not that Jennie could tell the difference, of course. She just thought I loved the movie.

About two-thirds of the way in, she ran to the ladies' room. My Blackberry had vibrated about 10 minutes earlier, but I had held off on checking it. I took a look. Lou Lamont had responded:

Interesting. Would love to hear more, but I need a name and a face. Don't worry. I'll keep your identity between us. Morton's is right near your building. How about we meet there at 12:30 tomorrow? You got an expense account at J&G?— LL

J&G was short for Jessup & Greer, which published *Currents*. In my anonymous email, I had claimed to be an insider at J&G who had in his possession an item that would disprove Mitch Blake's spin that *World*'s post-launch paging goals had always been in the modest 65- to 75-page range. The item was evidence, I had claimed, that *Mitch Blake has been feeding you nothing but lies for months, Mr. Lamont.*

I didn't like the thought of revealing my identity, however, or meeting in public. Morton's was too far from the Carlyle Nash offices to be a regular hangout for staffers, but a public meeting still meant taking the chance of running into a colleague. But I had an idea, and I wanted to move on it fast. Lamont's next column would run on Friday. His immediate response to my email suggested he was still looking for material as Thursday approached.

Jennie returned and asked me what she had missed. I told her, "Nothing important, one funny line," and said that I had to go the bathroom myself. When I reached the lobby, I made a phone call.

Keith picked up on the first ring. Heavy metal music was blaring in the background.

"Keith, it's Paul," I said. "You want to make some money?" ▪

CHAPTER TWENTY-TWO

Thursday
(2007)

I COULDN'T SLEEP, so when my Blackberry buzzed at two in the morning, I heard it. I rolled off my air mattress and got up to search in the darkness for my slacks. I found them on the floor and located the phone in a back pocket. I hit a key and the screen glowed. I sat down on the floor.

Mitch had emailed.

Paul—About today: Obviously, I didn't know about the situation you were dealing with. My condolences on the passing of your uncle. As hard as we go around here, family is still the most important thing. I would have understood had you told me. I want you to take tomorrow and Friday off and, if need be, any time you need next week. The magazine will be here when you get back. I'll check in with you on Monday to see how you're doing. The meeting went fine after you left. —Best, Mitch

I read the email again as I moved to the card table in the kitchen. I dissected every sentence, but I homed in on the final one.

"The meeting went fine after you left"? I don't give a shit how the meeting went, Mitch. Fucking ninjas could have dropped from the ceiling and slaughtered everyone at the table and I wouldn't care,

OK? Oh, and I get what you mean by "after you left." You're saying, "after what you did to my meeting, Paul." Do you think I'm stupid, Mitch? And "family is still the most important thing"? Bullshit. That's a cut-and-paste response you keep handy for when a staffer is heading to a wake. If I told you my goldfish died, you'd probably say "Few things are more important than our aquatic loved ones." Fuck you, motherfucker. Because of you, I'm living in a dump and sleeping on a raft.

I started to throw the Blackberry across the room but stopped myself. I crossed the kitchen and stood seething in front of the toaster oven. I had never punched anything in my life and thought Keith was a moron for ramming his fist into his windshield, but a perfect storm of anger, frustration, and morbid curiosity drove my right fist forward. The toaster oven's glass panel shattered as my fist powered through to the edge of the rusted center rack, opening a gash across my knuckles that immediately began oozing blood. I grabbed a wad of paper towels and pressed them against my hand. It didn't hurt as much as I thought it would, but I resisted the urge to hit something else. I checked the time on my Blackberry—2:10 AM—and opened the fridge. I cracked a beer and told myself that this is when second-shift workers start drinking.

The phone rang. It was Keith.

"What the fuck are you doing up there!?"

"Fuck off, Keith," I shouted. "Go back to bed and be ready for tomorrow."

"Don't make me evict your ass, Paul."

"Yeah right. I'm your fucking gravy train right now. I'll take that grand-a-month I'm paying you and spend it on a cheap motel."

"Big talk. Hey, speaking of a grand, I want the money for tomorrow upfront."

"No way. Best I'll do is five hundred in the morning and then five hundred after Morton's. And you only get the second five hundred if you don't fuck things up."

"OK. But you're paying for my train ticket too."

"Fine. Go back to bed. I'll be down at eight to go over the plan."

"OK, but keep it down up there. Don't fuck up my house."

"Too late. You've done a good job of that yourself. Sweet dreams, slumlord."

We both hung up. He screamed, "Night, asshole!" through the floorboards, loud enough to shake the card table. I drank the last two beers in the fridge, dialed Diane but hung up, watched an infomercial on kids starving in Africa, called the toll-free number and sponsored a kid from Zambia, and passed out.

* * * *

I CALLED KEITH TO WAKE HIM UP at 7:45. He asked what "my fucking problem" had been a few hours earlier, so I explained and apologized—the toaster oven had come with the apartment.

"I'll replace it," I said.

"Don't worry about it."

"Do you have any gauze?"

"Yeah. I got plenty of that shit. Come on down."

It was raining hard as I walked down the exterior staircase, so I let it beat down on my hand to get the blood-clotted paper towels to fall off. Without Diane there wielding a bottle of peroxide, this qualified as prepping the wound. Thankfully, Keith was surprisingly adept at cleaning and bandaging—despite his own still-wrapped hand. As he completed the job over his kitchen sink, I thanked and complimented him.

"Not bad," I said. "You're like a medic."

"I took some EMT classes. Pay was gonna suck though. So I started doing AC with my father. That was that."

He took six Eggo blueberry waffles out of the toaster and I ran him through the day's plan as we ate. I was paying him way too much money, of course, but, then again, asking a roughneck like Keith to convince a media columnist that he's in some way connected to Jessup & Greer was a tall order. As I watched him smear butter on a waffle with a soup spoon, I wondered again if this was a good idea. But I came to the same conclusion I had arrived at when the idea had first struck: *he may not be perfect, but he's far enough away from the industry that there's little risk of anyone connecting us.* After I drilled him on every answer to every potential question from Lou Lamont, I focused on his look.

"What would it take for you to shave that thing?"

He defensively stroked his thick, horseshoe-shaped trucker moustache. I cringed at the site of a new tattoo on the back of his left hand and remembered what John always said: *Every visible tattoo lowers your perceived IQ by ten points.* If that was true, Keith's perceived IQ was negative 3000. Each arm was covered from shoulder to wrist in a schizoid jigsaw of bald eagles, rifles, crosses, roses, and serpents. One or two inkings were fresh, most faded.

"No fucking way," he said. "The moustache stays. I've had this since I was thirteen."

"Alright, but you have a suit, right? Or at least a long-sleeved dress shirt?"

He sneered and left the room. I heard him opening and closing his closet. When he returned he was carrying a freshly pressed black pinstripe suit. It looked like it had cost as much as one of Simon's.

"Nice," I said.

"I know. I ain't a fucking savage, dude."

I laughed as I imagined what a conversation between him and Emily might sound like. I stood up.

"I'm gonna take a shower. Meet you out front in forty minutes."

As I scrambled up the stairs with my bandaged hand in a plastic bag, I could hear my phone ringing inside. I rushed in and answered without looking at the caller ID.

"Hello?"

"Paul…it's Diane."

I sat down and tried to catch my breath.

"Diane. Sorry, I was downstairs talking to Keith."

"I thought you'd be at work by now."

"No, I took the day off."

I waited for her to crack wise about how I never took days off before she left, but she just said, "Oh."

"I'm glad you called," I said.

"I'm returning your call. Last night. The hang-up?"

"Right. Yes, that was me. I'm sorry. I was just checking to see—"

"I would have talked to you, Paul. What's going on?"

"Nothing," I said. "I mean, well, I had a really bad day yesterday. Please don't get mad when I tell you this, but I really did skip the funeral because of work."

"Of course you did," she said in a flat tone.

"I asked you not to get mad."

"I'm not mad. I'm just...you know. You know how I feel, Paul."

"I do know. But listen, the day was an absolute disaster. I crashed and burned during a presentation. I walked out on Mitch. It's over. If I don't fuck it up, I'm going to go to work with John. Like you wanted. But I just have some loose ends to tie up first."

She was silent.

"Diane?"

"You really crashed and burned? Where? How?"

"It was at an offsite meeting upstate. I got completely hammered."

"You were drunk!?"

"No, no, no. I mean Mitch hammered me for answers I didn't have. It was awful. I even cried."

"Good."

"Good?"

"Something like that needed to happen."

I wasn't so sure, but I let it pass.

"How is Aidan?"

"He's fine. Don't worry about him."

"I do miss him, you know. I miss you."

"I know. But I want you to do something for me. My sister gave me the name of a therapist. She's in the city. I want you to see her. It's good that you're going to work with John, but I know you. Before long, it'll be Simon this and Simon that. And I'm not even talking about how it would affect me. It's about you. You can't do this to yourself anymore. I know you and John drink too much together—that needs to change too—but at least with him it's...work hard, play hard. I hate that stupid phrase, but it's appropriate here. The majority of people do their job, leave it at the office, and go home to their loved ones..."

"But what about getting ahead, Diane? I'm not sure that—"

"Please let me finish, Paul. They work hard and maybe they play hard too. But then they go home to be with their loved ones. And when they're with their loved ones, they're *with* their loved ones. And when they're not with them, they at least think about them once in a while and consider how their behavior will affect them."

She paused. I had no response.

"You know, Paul...I was remembering the other day about that time when you first started working at *Bellwether* and I had an early-morning job interview in Mineola. You dropped me off on your way to the train, and you knew I'd have to take a bus home because my car was in the shop. Remember what you did? You didn't go to work that day. You sat in the car and waited until I finished the interview so you could drive me home. That's the man I fell in love with."

I considered defending myself. We had been newlyweds then. I was just starting out. I could do things like that then. Nobody even knew who I was. But once Mitch came on board and then Michael started bringing me into meetings...

Diane was silent, waiting.

"Send me the therapist's name," I said.

"You'll call her?"

"I will. Can I stop over this weekend?"

She hesitated.

"Make the appointment, first. See the therapist. Then we'll pick a day in a week or two. OK?"

"OK. I love you, Diane."

"I love you too. Please just try to relax today."

"I'll try."

* * * *

KEITH'S SUIT TURNED OUT to be a size too small, so I had to help him out of his jacket when we arrived at Morton's at 11:45 a.m., well ahead of his 12:15 p.m. Lou Lamont meeting time.

"Hurry up," he said as I yanked it by the collar from behind with my good left hand. "I don't want anyone thinking we're a fucking couple."

"You're not my type."

He reversed the inside-out sleeves and folded the jacket over his arm. I was dressed casually in khakis, a red polo shirt, and a U.S Open golf cap, and kept my bandaged right hand in my pants pocket. We entered together, pretending to be acquaintances who had just bumped into each other but were there separately, each expecting a guest. We arrived early enough to secure adjacent high tables in the front bar section. That way, I could sit back-to-back with Keith and listen in on his conversation with Lamont. I planned to eventually tell my waiter that my guest got tied up at the office so I would be dining alone. I pulled my hat low over my eyes as I sat down, in case a Carlyle Nash colleague happened to walk in. It was unlikely, but there was always a mild risk.

In a confirming email to Lamont, I had told him to look for *the guy in a pinstriped suit with a trucker moustache.* He had replied, *OK. I guess J&G is loosening up these days.*

I sipped my water and passed the time reading and responding to other emails that were mostly from people at *World* asking how I was doing after my meltdown. *Better*, I answered. *Thanks for asking*. As usual, Lily and Matt were keeping things under control at the office—although Lily reminded me that she had a vacation scheduled for the following week. I told her not to worry and that I would come in on Monday. I needed to be there anyway in case Simon's offer came as scheduled.

"You want a beer?" Keith asked behind me.

"Don't talk to me, Keith," I said without turning. "We're not together."

"The guy's not even here yet."

"Just order your own drink from the waiter. Forget you know me."

He turned around in his stool.

"Hey," he said. "You forgot to give me a credit card. I ain't paying for this asshole's lunch."

"Oh yeah. Take this instead."

I slipped him three $100 bills.

"If he comments about you paying with cash," I added, "just say you don't want a paper trail."

"Got it."

The waiter approached my table first. I hid my bandaged hand under the table.

"Would you like something from the bar, sir?"

"Yes, thanks. I'll have a glass of cabernet."

Keith chuckled derisively.

"Oh man," he muttered.

The waiter moved to his table.

"And you, sir. Can I get you a drink?"

"Give me a Busch," he said proudly.

"I'm sorry, sir. I'm afraid we don't serve Busch."

"Unbelievable. Busch Light then."

"I'm afraid we don't stock that either. How about a Stella?"

"Fine, whatever," said Keith. "Some steakhouse. A guy can't get the best beer in America."

The waiter left.

"Jesus, Keith," I said. "Can you please act like you've been in a restaurant other than fucking IHOP."

"You ever have a steak at IHOP? Don't knock it, man."

"No, I haven't. Now please, stop talking to me and don't laugh when I order a glass of wine."

"Alright, alright. Enjoy your chick drink. Surprised you didn't get a Cosmotini."

The lunch crowd began arriving and I kept an eye out for Lou Lamont, hoping he still looked roughly like the photo that had been running atop his column for nearly a decade. I was prepared for an older, fatter, balder incarnation.

Just as my wine arrived, a bushy-haired, fiftyish man in rumpled gray khakis, white sneakers, and a blue polo shirt passed by the restaurant's front window and entered. It was him. I watched as he headed toward the main dining room. The host was talking to another party, so he slipped by in search of a trucker moustache. I whispered to Keith, "Be ready, he's here." A few seconds later, he came back out into the bar. Keith turned and looked at him and Lou walked over. Lamont wiped his right hand on his pants as he walked up.

Stand up, Keith.

He didn't. Lamont extended his hand.

"You must be the, uh, savage," he said. "Or maybe I should call you the trucker."

I cringed as Keith didn't respond at all. I pictured the vacant look on his face as he failed to make the connection to my email handle, which I *had* prepped him on.

"OK," said Lamont. "A man of few words."

The waiter descended immediately and Lamont ordered a scotch and water.

"My name is Randy," said Keith. "What should I call you?"

"Lou is fine. Nice to meet you."

"Likewise."

As Lou took his seat the waiter approached me.

"You'll still be two for lunch, sir?"

I kept my bandaged hand under the table.

"Just canceled," I said. "Looks like I'll be eating alone. I'll have a Caesar salad and the filet, medium-rare. Baked potato with butter. Thanks."

"Certainly. Sorry you'll be dining alone..."

I strained to hear what Keith was saying behind me, but the waiter kept talking as he cleared the second place setting at my table.

"...but sometimes single dining experiences turn out to be the best meals. I was visiting a friend in Chicago recently and he had to cancel..."

Oh, you've got to be kidding me. Me and my friendly fucking face.

"...at the last minute. I was at Lawry's Prime Rib, at one of their against-the-wall tables facing the whole restaurant..."

He paused and smiled. "Have you ever been there, sir?"

Keith and Lamont began laughing behind me.

"So fucking right, dude," Keith said.

The waiter was waiting for my response. I answered in the unfriendliest tone I could muster.

"Yes, I have."

It didn't work.

"Then you know what I'm talking about. You'd think you would feel strange sitting at a table alone and facing about sixty people, but it's actually quite nice. Great people-watching, and the food is out of this world."

"Right," I said. "I liked it too."

My Blackberry blessedly vibrated on the table and I grabbed it. The message was spam, but I pretended it was important. The waiter picked up on my body language.

"I'll bring your Caesar salad," he said.

"Thanks."

"If you would just hand me that menu? I don't want to reach across."

"Of course."

Please fucking go. Please.
"And can I get you another glass of wine, sir?"
"I'm OK…yeah, sure, you can bring me another. Thanks."
"My pleasure. I'll be back with that in a moment."
Keith laughed again.
"I would fuck that right in half."
Thankfully it seemed I hadn't missed anything important. They were ogling a drop-dead gorgeous blond who had taken a seat at the bar a few minutes earlier.
"Definitely," said Lamont. "Wouldn't need a blue pill for that."
Keith responded with his mouth full.
"This bread is awesome. Have a piece."
The waiter returned with Lamont's scotch and another beer for Keith. Lamont said his time was limited, so they placed their steak orders. He asked Keith to pass the butter.
"So anyway, Randy. What's your last name?"
Keith paused again. I sensed him tensing up as he consulted his mental cue cards.
"Randy K. Just Randy K."
"Randy Kaye? Like Danny Kaye?"
"Not Danny. Randy."
"I know that," said Lamont with a chuckle. "I'm asking if your last name is Kaye, K-A-Y-E. Or is it K-A-Y like the Yankees announcer?"
"No man. It's just an initial. We're not giving a last name."
This is the dumbest idea I've ever had.
Lamont paused.
"What do you mean by *we're* not giving a last name? Who's 'we,' Randy?"
"Me and my guy. The guy. The guy from Jessup and Green who asked me to meet with you."
Jessup and Greer, you idiot.
"Oh, well that explains a lot. So you're not with J and G? I thought from the emails that I'd be meeting with Savage Marketer Nine himself. Who exactly are you?"

"I'm your worst fucking nightmare."

I clenched my napkin.

What the hell are you doing, Keith!?

"Excuse me?" asked Lamont in amazement and what sounded like mild fear.

Keith began laughing.

"I'm just fucking with you, man. You know, this is like a spy movie or something. And you're the bad guy."

Lamont laughed nervously.

"Who *are* you? Really?"

"Oh man. You looked like you were gonna shit. No, really, my name is Randy. I do electrical work at J and G's building—contract stuff—and I became really good friends with someone who works directly for the, uh, the boss...the publisher...of the magazine..."

Currents, Currents, Currents, Keith.

"...*Currents*."

"Dennis Cameron?" asked Lamont.

"Who?"

"Dennis Cameron. He's the publisher of *Currents*."

"Yeah, right. My buddy works for him. So anyway, my buddy got his hands on the beach ball and he—oh man, what the fuck, he, uhh. Right, right, right—he doesn't want to be the guy to give it you, but it's something that's important to his boss."

"So this is coming from Cameron? Indirectly?"

"That I don't know. But I'm here because none of them want you to know who they are."

Lamont sighed.

"OK, I've used anonymous sources before, but I just need to verify that this thing is real and that... Wait a minute, you have this beach ball and card on you, right?"

"Oh yeah, I got that."

My Caesar salad arrived as I heard Keith reaching back into the breast pocket of his suit for the deflated beach ball. As he searched for it, an open package of Red Man chewing tobacco—wrapped in a thick rubber band—fell to the floor and kicked directly under my feet. I had no choice but to act natural. I picked it up and handed it to him over my shoulder, without turning my head around.

"Thank you…sir," said Keith.

I cringed and buried myself in my salad, chewing softly so I could hear. Keith handed Lamont the beach ball, to which I had reattached the incentive card with duct tape. Lamont laughed.

"One hundred and fifty ad pages? That was Blake's original target? That lying fuck has been telling me seventy-five was their high-end all along. And I kept printing his bullshit. The September issue will close at eighty, and from what I've heard, October is going to be as thin as Kate Moss. Hilarious."

Keith was silent.

"You have no idea what I'm talking about, do you Randy?"

"Nope. I'm just the messenger, man."

Keith continued chewing on bread in silence as Lamont typed on his phone. I assumed he was making notes. As I sipped my wine, I thought that the operation might just work after all. Lamont stopped typing.

"Can I blow it up?"

"Go ahead, man."

Three deep breaths later, the beach ball was inflated. He laughed as the steaks arrived. Keith laughed along.

"This is some stupid shit, right bro?"

"It is. Hey, can I take a picture of this?"

Keith was silent.

Yes, Keith, yes. Let him take a picture, you idiot.

He leaned far back on his stool. The back of his head was nearly touching mine.

Yes, yes, yes, yes, yes.

He leaned forward again.

"Yeah, I got no problem with that."

I exhaled as Lamont took multiple photos of the ball and card. *Click-click, click-click.*

Keith dug into his steak as mine arrived.

"So," he asked, "why do you have such a hard-on for this Mitch dude?"

He had grossly reworded my question, but it was something I was curious about.

"Listen," said Lamont as he cut into his steak. "when you write a media column, people spin you all the time. I get it. That's the game. And half the time, I need the material to fill space anyway. But Mitch Blake takes it to a new level. I'm just tired of being used by him and by Carlyle Nash in general. I started to question my own integrity a bit after..."

He paused and sipped his drink.

"You're not following, are you?"

"Right again, man. It was just something my buddy wanted to know."

"Oh, OK. Well...good luck explaining it back to him then."

"Yeah, yeah. I got it. I got the general idea."

Shut up, Keith. Let him talk. He started to question his own integrity after what? Fuck. Let him finish his thought.

"So tell me more about your buddy. What does he do at J and G?"

The moment was gone.

"He works with the ads and shit. I don't know. Writes them."

"He *writes* the ads?"

"Something like that. He writes everything there."

Stop, Keith. Please stop.

"Hmmm. OK. Well, that's not usually the way the business works. Advertisers typically—"

"We don't talk much business."

"Can you give me his name? I promise it'll stay between you and me."

"No names, man, no names. This steak is fucking great, by the way."

"How about just a first name?"

"I call him Hemingway. It's a nickname. You know, 'cause he's a writer."

"Right. A writer. Who works for the publisher. Not the editor?"

"I have no idea what you're asking, man."

Lamont laughed again.

"Alright, alright. Don't worry about it. I'm gonna move on this. This beach ball looks for real—pure Carlyle Nash excess. That company pretty much exists to waste money."

"That's what my buddy says about the place."

Oh no. Oh no.

"About Carlyle Nash?"

"Right. Cause he...you know. He just knows everything about everything."

"Well, OK. Interesting. Mitch Blake has a lot of enemies right inside those walls, so it's always fun to figure out who's plotting against whom. Where do you live, Randy?"

"I live in Hicksville, man."

"You don't have a buddy at Carlyle Nash too, do you?"

"I do not."

Lamont excused himself to go to the men's room.

"How am I doing?" asked Keith.

"Later," I said.

My table was facing the men's room, so when Lamont returned, I hunched down low over my near-finished steak but sensed a stare as he passed. He ate the last of his steak standing up.

"Alright, Randy. I'm on deadline, so I have to run. Tell your buddy—the Savage, that is—that I appreciate the lead and that I'll email him if I have any questions. Thanks for lunch. He bankrolled you for this, right?"

"Yeah, I got it, man. Good meeting you."

"Good luck with that."

Lamont must have been gesturing to the blond at the bar.

"In my dreams, man."

Lamont exited. As he passed by the front window, I wiped my mouth with my napkin and whispered to Keith,

"Don't turn around yet. Don't turn around yet."

Lamont seemed to give me a fleeting glance, before trotting across 45th Street.

"Solid, right?" asked Keith.

I exhaled.

"Yeah, Keith. I guess so." ▪

CHAPTER TWENTY-THREE

Friday
(2007)

I WOKE UP THE NEXT MORNING with a feeling of certainty: Mitch would know it was me. The time was 7:55 AM, so he would probably be in the office by now—he liked to jam as much work into a Summer Friday as any other day. Naomi would be bringing in his tabbed morning reads in a few minutes, and the first one he would turn to would be Lou Lamont's column. I sat up on my air mattress and began rocking nervously. By 10:00 AM, the Carlyle Nash building would be rocking too. On every floor and at every magazine, the question would be "Did you read Lamont today!?" I could already feel the tremors caused by the column's takeaway: Mitch Blake wasn't beating September's ad-page target by five pages; he was falling short by a staggering 70. *World* Magazine was a one-hit wonder and it was going under, fast.

Mitch would be in full damage-control mode already, but determining who leaked the beach-ball story would be just as important to him—maybe even more important. He would be coming for me. I grabbed my Blackberry to do some damage control of my own:

Mitch—I can't tell you how much I appreciate your email. I hope you understand my delayed response, but after the offsite, I obviously needed to step away from things for a day or two. I appreciate the days off. With some time to think, I'm already feeling a bit better. That said, I may indeed take you up on the offer of a few more days next week to focus on myself and my family—but only if it's convenient for you. I'll be in on Monday, and we can decide then. There's still important work ahead and I remain a big believer in World—*but I do know that the most important work I need to do right now is on myself. I'm grateful for your understanding. Thanks and best, Paul.*

"Blah, blah, blabbedy bullshit," I sang as I sent the message off. If indeed Mitch was on to me, this was the right tack: throw him off with the message that Paul is focusing on himself right now—and as loyal as he's always been and still is, he would never dream of committing such a betrayal.

Now that I thought about it, perhaps it wasn't such a certainty that Mitch knew. Maybe he had, in fact, ruled me out a long time ago and was presently running down the names on the *World* phone list for suspects to interrogate. But it really didn't matter to me anymore. The column had hit and I was ready for the consequences. In the worst scenario, I could sling hash right up the corner at the Hicksville Deli. *Bacon, egg, and cheese? Home fries with that? Coming right up.*

I pulled on a T-shirt and pair of shorts, slipped into flip-flops, and headed out to pick up the *Tribune*. I visualized how the beach ball and incentive card photos might look and briefly wondered if it would be possible for anyone to determine that the shot had been taken at Morton's. I pictured the grain of the tabletop before deciding that I was completely overthinking things again. But as I walked along the block's neglected sidewalks—weeds sprouting up from fissures and fault lines—I began to worry about the furtive glance Lamont had given me when he left the restaurant.

What if he figured out that I was listening in all along? What if he surreptitiously snapped a photo of me too? What if I didn't have my hat pulled down low enough? What if...the photo in the column isn't a picture of the beach ball but of me? I could see the headline: "Mole at Morton's: Mitch Blake's Double-Crossing Director."

I sprinted the rest of the way.

Next door to the deli was a stationery store that had been run by an old Pakistani couple when Diane and I had lived in the neighborhood. I recognized them as I entered to the sound of jingling door chimes. The wife was dusting a display of cheap greeting cards. The husband was behind the counter writing winning lottery numbers on a dry-erase board. She didn't seem to recognize me, but he did.

"Hello there," he said. "Long time."

I paused to catch my breath.

"Hi. Yes, I'm back visiting a friend in the neighborhood. Just stopping in for a newspaper. Do you still sell the *Tribune*?"

"Yes. I don't like their politics much, but people want it, so..."

"I just read it for the sports section."

I spotted a copy on the rack and picked it up. The front page blared news of a suicide attempt by Owen Wilson. I wondered by what method. The smell of cigars wafted from the partially open self-serve humidor, so I grabbed four Macanudo Portofinos for the lonely weekend ahead. As I paid up, I was hoping not to have to make too much small talk.

"Good to see you," I said. "I'll be back in the area a bit more, so I'll come in again."

"You too, sir. Enjoy your rest."

Enjoy my rest? Well, at least he didn't tell me I looked tired.

A pair of white plastic tables with weathered Corona Light umbrellas were set out in front of the deli. I brushed a gum wrapper off a chair and sat down. I paged quickly to the business section. As usual, Lou Lamont's mug stared back from the lower half of page B5...but there was no accompanying photo of the beach ball. The column's headline read: "Jessup & Greer Acquires Schrank Enthusiast Group." I ran my finger across to a shorter secondary news item, but it too had nothing to do with *World* or Carlyle Nash. I paged backwards to see if the beach ball story had run as a separate lead article, but the business section led with a report on recessionary fears on Wall Street. I tried not to overreact.

OK. So he missed his deadline. He went back to the office after lunch and tried to work a few other inside sources at Carlyle Nash to see if the story held water. By the time he verified everything, it was too late, so he's holding the piece for Tuesday. Simple explanation. I just have to remain patient.

This was better, in fact, because Lamont's Tuesday column was more widely read than his Friday one, when so many senior Carlyle Nashers were off to the Hamptons for the weekend. Better if the bombshell hit on Tuesday, when they were all back at their desks. But I wanted verification, so I reached into my shorts for my Blackberry. I typed a simple *Holding for Tuesday?* in the subject line and sent the message off from the Savage address. Lamont responded within a minute, and we volleyed back and forth:

Lamont: *Yes. Sort of.*

Savage: *Sort of?*

Lamont: *Working on some new developments.*

Savage: *Can you share?*

Lamont: *Cannot.*

Savage: *Maybe in person?*

Lamont: *With you?*

Savage: *How about Randy?*

Lamont: *Quite a guy, but I want the Savage. I'm sure you have more to share.*

Savage: *Yes, but I need to think about that.*

Lamont: *Must be by Monday afternoon latest.*

Savage: *No reveal of my identity, correct?*

Lamont: *Correct.*

Savage: *I'll be in touch.*

I moved my chair under the umbrella as a light rain began

to fall. I didn't know how to feel. Even though I had initially been disappointed that the article hadn't run, I also felt a faint sense of relief. If Lamont decided to forego the story completely, I would still have the beach ball. I still *had* the beach ball, of course, but in revealing it to him, I had for the first time ceded total control of it. Oddly, the part of me that wanted that control back was now in effective opposition to the part that wanted to unleash the beach ball on Mitch's reputation. And then there was the small voice that had periodically piped up since I first concocted this scheme, asking the same question each time: "Have you lost your fucking mind, Paul?"

An email arrived from John.

Hey — I know you're out, but you have to get to the city for lunch with me and Simon. Let's get this done. Simon said it can't wait until Monday. The Sichuan place in Hell's Kitchen at 1.

I picked up egg sandwiches for me and Keith and sprinted back.

* * * *

I ARRIVED AT THE RESTAURANT in my best suit and with my hair combed in the traditional side part. Neither had ever failed me before. I was 20 minutes late because of a train delay, but only John had arrived. The restaurant was full and a bit loud, owing to poor acoustics. John sat at a large, round table—way too big for three people—in the very center of the room. A bottle of Tsingtao beer and a glass sat in front of him. The table was empty but for a gleaming white tablecloth.

"Intimate," I shouted. "Is this so I'll miss clauses in the offer?"

"I forgot to make a reservation. Simon will be pissed."

He tugged the sleeve of a passing waiter and pointed to his beer.

"Same for my friend, please."

"I don't get a choice?" I asked.

"Drink what Simon drinks today."

I took my jacket off and settled in.

"So today's the day. Am I going to be happy?"

"Very happy."

Although it sounded like a done deal, and my mind was made up, my heart still beat quickly in anticipation of my first major career decision since leaving *Bellwether*.

"Here he is," said John.

Simon made his usual regal entrance and headed for the table. I stood up to shake his hand, but he gave John an angry look and began scanning the room. The restaurant's owner hurried over. They shook hands and began speaking in Mandarin. I sat back down. The owner snapped his fingers to a pair of waiters and barked an order. Simon gestured to John and me.

"Up," he said.

We stood, and the waiters carried the table away and brought a small square replacement. Simon bade me to sit.

"Please, Paul."

"Thank you, Simon."

John circled to my side and took the seat next to me.

"Sorry, Simon," he said. "Reservation mix-up."

"Clearly," said Simon as he sat directly across from me. "But these things can be fixed quickly, as you see."

"I see," I said.

He spread his napkin on his lap.

"So, Paul. How's your new love?"

I had expected him to rib me about Jennie at some point, but not right away. I laughed nervously.

"It's really not like that. And if I've insulted you in any way by spending time with her—"

"Insulted me? Not at all, mate. Listen, my dalliance with the fair Jennie was really just a pair of friends hugging too hard a few times. I do want the best for her. And she seems to want you."

"She said that?"

"Not it in so many words, but a man can tell."

"We really are just friends, but I suppose—"

A waiter arrived with Tsingtaos for Simon and me. John ordered several starters. Simon sipped his beer and wiped his beard with his napkin.

"Well, mate, friends or something more, she seems to think you're pretty wonderful. Make of it what you will."

"And you're OK with that?"

"You have my blessing."

He took an envelope from his breast pocket and slid it across to me.

"So," he continued. "Young man walks into a restaurant. He walks out with the right to court a beautiful woman, and...a thirty percent increase in salary."

I turned to John and he smiled. I picked up the envelope and opened it. Simon noticed my bandaged hand, but I had a feeling he wouldn't ask about it.

From the job title to the eye-popping salary and bonus structure, it was more than I had expected. I considered the ridiculousness of the timing. Forty-eight hours earlier I had been an emotional mess in the mountains. Should I just forget about that? Or should I man up and discuss it?

"This is incredibly generous, Simon."

"Your work and your reputation merit it. And I think you're up for the challenge."

"I believe I am too, but I have to ask one thing."

"By all means."

I took a deep breath and a sip of my beer.

"Two days ago—at an offsite meeting for *World*—I had a pretty public meltdown. Actually very public..."

John shifted uncomfortably next to me, as if I need not go into the story.

"...I was dealing with a death in my family and my presentation was also thrown off by some miscommunication on tech needs. It got to a point that Mitch—"

"I heard about it, mate."

"You did? How?"

"It's not important, Paul," John interjected. "We've talked about it. Shit happens."

"Just ask John," said Simon. "He flipped a table or two back in the day. One time he didn't have his pants on."

John smiled and shook his head.

"Well, OK." I said with relief. "I guess it's all going to work out. I suppose I just have to give notice to Mitch."

"If you think it necessary, mate. But the current Carlyle HR policy is 'open season' when it comes to internal candidates. We can seal this deal right now…and then you can simply share the news of your decision with Mitch."

I looked down at the offer sheet in disbelief.

"Then I guess this calls for a toast."

Simon smiled.

"In a minute. I do have just one small condition which I hope you'll agree to."

"Of course. What is it?"

He picked up a just-arrived steamed dumpling with a pair of chopsticks.

"You'll need to give me the beach ball."

He looked me in the eyes as he chewed slowly. I was silent for a good ten seconds as I tried my best to maintain eye contact. I couldn't tell if he knew for certain that I had it or if he was bluffing, trying to psych me out. But I knew immediately what his intentions were.

He wants to use the beach ball against Mitch. If the Morelands know about it, he can gain a leg up with them in the process. And maybe he even intends to share it with Lou Lamont himself.

I was still holding the offer letter. As I formulated my do-or-die response, I remembered something my dad used to say: *Don't do anyone's dirty work. Keep your hands clean.* That didn't necessarily mean I wanted to abandon my own efforts to smear Mitch in the press. I just didn't like the idea of playing the rat in an internal power struggle. Simon was asking me to do something that felt far more nefarious than what I had been up to myself. It was a dirty deal and I was the guy in the dark alley rooting through a trash can for Simon's sack of money. Worse, maybe he didn't even care what talents and abilities I might bring to the job. He knew about my meltdown; maybe he thought I was damaged goods. Perhaps my primary value to him *was* the beach ball. As I looked down at the letter, Emily's putdown rang in my ears: *You're one job removed from slinging hash somewhere, aren't you?* But it didn't feel like a putdown to me now. It felt like a compliment.

"I don't have a beach ball, Simon. I gave mine back to Mitch when he asked for it."

John put his hands to his face. Simon smiled.

"I think you know which beach ball I'm talking about. Come on, mate. I'm just going to have some fun with it."

I looked at John, but he didn't look back. I had a sinking feeling that he had finally told Simon everything I'd confided to him at Del Frisco's—or, if not told him outright, had at least confirmed Simon's suspicions that I had the ball. It was probably foolish to continue to deny it since I'd already shared the beach ball with Lamont, but something still made me hold back.

At the same time, however, another weakening part of me was quietly calculating the difference in take-home that a 30 percent raise would yield. My net would be roughly three times as much as my father had ever earned. I wondered what he would do in my situation. I visualized him sitting at the dining room table with a stack of bills, consulting a pen-and-ink budget he kept on an index card. Nine kids...and he still found a way to buy me a used car.

I didn't have to wonder too long.

"I'm sorry, Simon. I don't know what beach ball you're talking about."

He put down his dumpling and laughed.

"You're kidding me, right?"

I pushed the envelope back across the table.

"Maybe I am. I'm sorry, but this is between me and someone else. I hope you understand."

"I really don't."

I stood up, put on my suit jacket and turned to John.

"I'll talk to you next week." ▪

CHAPTER TWENTY-FOUR

Sunday-Monday
(2007)

IF THERE'S ANYTHING I'm stubborn about—and I'm stubborn about plenty—it's not entertaining on Sundays. Even as a kid, the presence of friends or relatives at the house on the day before a school day was not my idea of fun. Life's pressures and responsibilities lurked with the dawn, and the last thing I wanted to do was make chitchat during my waning hours of freedom. My father had been the same way. Like him, I preferred to spend Sundays wallowing in quiet misery. It had been a source of frustration for Diane, but she accommodated me by scheduling weekend social events on Fridays and Saturdays only—which also allowed me to sleep in on Sundays after a second night of drinking.

I thought about this when I returned from Sunday lunch at my mother's house and had to make my way through the 40 or 50 members of Keith's motorcycle club who had invaded the back yard following a trip to Jones Beach. I had finally worked up the nerve at lunch to tell my mother about the separation from Diane. But Diane had already told her. In fact, the name of the therapist Diane had asked me to call hadn't come from her sister but from mine. It was a white lie I supposed I could forgive, but I nevertheless looked forward to bringing it up with Diane. My mother had added that nearly all my siblings—at least the ones who weren't mad at me—had offered up the names of therapists or priests. I hadn't realized how concerned they were. But I guess when you shut your loved ones out of your life for a year and cap it off by skipping a family funeral, they tend to notice. Still, I wasn't ready to talk to them yet. I needed more time. I'd made an appointment with the therapist, and I wasn't looking forward to that, either. But I had promised Diane.

Keith didn't see me as I slipped past. He had a leather-clad lady friend pinned up against the house's rotting rear siding. She held a red plastic cup of beer pressed against her thigh as he licked her neck and ground his pelvis against hers. Camelot it wasn't. Across the yard, two of his buddies were lifting another biker by his arms and legs and threatening to throw him into Keith's neglected, algae-covered, above-ground pool. I didn't wait to see how things turned out.

When I got inside the apartment, I checked the refrigerator for food, hoping I wouldn't have to go back down the stairs to buy dinner. Fortunately, there was a box of Ellio's pizza in the freezer and half a liter of tonic water on the counter. Good enough, and it would be smart to dry out after spending the past two nights drinking gin and smoking cigars out on the staircase—alone with my unquiet mind.

The question I had wrestled with on both nights remained unanswered: What do I do now? I'd made my move on the beach ball thinking that once the shit hit the fan for Mitch, I would be on my way to Corporate. That wasn't happening now. Even if I broke down and called Simon on Monday, I had a feeling that offer was off the table. The look on his face when I left the restaurant had been one of offense and instant contempt. I had insulted the throne.

So it was with a combination of sadness and fear that I looked ahead to my return to *World* the next day. While Mitch was sure not to renege on his offer of additional time off—who would want me around anyway, so soon after my embarrassing display?—I knew that before long the familiar frustrating dynamic between us would return: my obsessive need to please him banging up against his sphinxlike nature and frugal parceling of praise. The only thing that could save me from a return to "normal" was the beach ball. I desperately wanted to know if Lamont planned to run with it. Should I reveal myself as the Savage on Monday and find out? Or should I just quietly wait for his Tuesday column? I wrestled with the choice all the way through extra innings of ESPN Sunday Night Baseball—played at top volume to drown out Keith's bash. In the end, I decided that the smarter choice was to sit tight and wait. I would go into the office on Monday and Tuesday to tie up loose ends and make sure Matt could handle things while Lily was out before taking my leave from Wednesday through Friday. I couldn't be out Tuesday, because I didn't want to miss the fallout if Lamont's column hit.

As I was scrubbing burnt pizza cheese off a cookie sheet, my Blackberry vibrated from atop the broken toaster oven. I dried my hands and looked at the message. It was from Jennie. I worried that she might be angry, that Simon might have returned from lunch and lied to her: *Paul said you were a crashing bore, my dear.* But her email simply read *Movies tomorrow night?*

I sighed with relief and responded.

Sounds great, Jennie.

* * * *

THE GIRL KEITH HAD BEEN HUMPING was sunbathing in her bra and panties on my landing when I left for work in the morning. As I stepped around her chaise lounge to get to the stairs, she apologized and added that she had "wanted to get closer to the sun." I made a note to tell Keith that she was perfect for him.

I barely made the 7:33 train out of Hicksville. As I squeezed into a seat between two passengers, my Blackberry vibrated. I contorted myself to take it out of my pocket without elbowing my seatmates. The email was from Mitch, responding to my Friday response.

That's good to hear, Paul. I put a call in to Sarah Monk in HR. The company offers services and referrals if you need to talk to someone. She's expecting you at 3PM today and will take you through every-thing. I'm in outside meetings all morning and gone after that. Take the week. It will be good for you.

So this was how it was going to be? Send me to the out-patient nut farm, see if they could fix my brain, and then sideline me when I got back? I knew exactly what his outside meetings were all about: finding my replacement. Maybe Michael Pace was coming back after all. *Well fuck you, Mitch. I'm going out guns blazing.* I logged in as the Savage and fired off a message to Lamont: *Where and when? The beach ball is only the beginning.*

Then I waited. And waited. As the train descended into the tunnel and approached the final stretch to Penn Station, there was still no response.

Calm down, you idiot. He's probably banging away at his key-board right now. He's putting the finishing touches on the article. Or he's just having his morning coffee. Relax. He'll respond soon.

Lily was on vacation and Matt was at a training session, so I was able to head straight to my office without having to discuss my emotional state with anyone. I was also relieved that I still *had* an office. I'd yet to find out what office Mary Ellen was be-ing moved into, but no news was good news—and I supposed it didn't really matter anymore. My mind was focused on the beach ball.

John had left a voicemail. The time stamp was Friday at 10:20 PM, and he sounded like he'd had a few more drinks after I'd left him and Simon at the restaurant.

Hey…Paul. Still pretty stunned by what you did, but I think I get it. I just want you to know that I didn't offer the information to Simon. He asked me if I thought you had the beach ball and I said I did. That's it. I thought you would just hand it over. I figured you didn't give a shit about Mitch anymore. You'll have to explain that to me. Anyway, like I said, I think I know why you refused. Simon can be a real scumbag sometimes. And he's pretty paranoid right now. I think something's coming to a head with him and Mitch and the Morelands. Maybe. I don't fucking know. Just a feeling. A lot of closed doors and whispering around here lately. Call me on Monday. You're a good man. Better than me. One way or another, we'll work together again. That's if I even have a fucking job. Later.

I appreciated the call, but I had already decided to forgive him for whatever he'd said. The power Simon had over him wasn't much different than Mitch's power over me. I played the message back again, though, because I wanted to make sure I'd heard him right. Yes, he had said that Simon only *thought* I had the beach ball. If that was the case, I was glad to hear it. It meant I had been right to think Simon might be bluffing. It also meant that, even if I was a suspect, no one knew for a fact that I had the beach ball except John. And if Mitch suspected me, why wouldn't he have just confronted me by now? What did he really have to lose? Maybe I was in the clear after all. Maybe my meltdown and the revelations of what I was dealing with at home made Mitch even more convinced that I had way too much going on in my personal life right now to even contemplate plotting against him. I still harbored the mild fear that Lamont had a lead on my identity, but, deep down, I suspected that was just paranoia.

I spun my chair around and took a long look at the skyscrapers outside my window. My time in that prime office might be coming to an end, but I was once again feeling in control of the situation. *No one* was on to me...and even if someone was, I would just deny, deny, deny. Maybe when the story hit, I would even march into Mitch's office, curse the unknown perpetrator, and vow to find out who it was during my leave of absence. *You can count on me, Mitch. Let's find this bastard.*

But *would* the story hit? By midday, Lamont still hadn't responded to my email requesting a meeting.

With Lily and Matt both out, I was able to slip out of our office area quietly at lunch. If anyone needed any marketing help, well, too bad. I decided to kill time before my 3:00 PM meeting with HR by walking up to the therapist's office on 57th and Columbus to track the distance and see how long it would take.

* * * *

THE RECEPTION DESK on the HR floor was being manned by a thirtyish male temp. He didn't have much to do and seemed to want me to notice that he was reading *Respect for Acting* by Uta Hagen.

"I have an appointment with Sarah Monk," I said.

He shifted the book slowly from in front of his face but held it conspicuously aloft above his shoulder.

"Who should I tell her is here?"

"Paul Cavanaugh."

I could see that he was practically begging me to say something like, "So you're an actor? Good for you. Keep at it. This corporate life is awful." But I had seen his cloying, plaintive look on the faces of hundreds of aspiring actors when I had run auditions for murder-mystery dinner theater down in Deerfield. I wanted to tell him instead that 99.9% percent of actors don't make it, *so get comfortable at that desk, Brando,* but I gave him a pass and sat down.

Two chairs to my left sat a young woman who appeared to be a recent college graduate. She was wearing a smart black dress suit and her red hair was tied back tightly in a bun. She was diligently filling out a job application form, pressing down hard with her pencil against a clear Lucite clipboard, stopping occasionally to nervously chew the end of her pencil and think. I *did* want to tell *her* that the corporate world was awful. *You should try to be an actress. You have a great face. Follow your dream.*

A strand of hair dropped down in front of her face. She whispered, "Damn," and tried to put it back up, glancing up briefly and catching my stare. I looked away but continued watching her out of the corner of my eye. She went back to the form but immediately encountered what seemed like another difficult question. She looked at the watch on her left wrist as her right foot began to bounce up and down.

"You know," I said, "the only information that needs to be accurate on that form is your address and Social Security number. So you can get paid after you get the job."

It wasn't intended as a pick-up line but she nevertheless gave me a look that said, "Are you really trying to hit on me before my interview?"

"Thanks," she said, turning back to the form.

"I'm serious," I said. "It's all bullshit. Your references, your GPA, your extracurricular activities. Write down anything. They won't check. If you nail the interview and look the part, you'll get the job."

The thespian at reception buried his head deeper in his book, pretending not to be listening. He wasn't much of an actor.

She stared at me with her brow furrowed a bit, her mouth half-open.

"Do you work here?"

"I do."

"And you really think they won't check anything?"

"I don't *think* they won't. I *know* they won't. What's the question you're having trouble with?"

"Well, they want my work history. I just graduated, but I don't want to write N-A. Should I put down that I worked at Dairy Queen when I was a freshman?"

"Sure. But say you were promoted to night manager after two months. For the name of your direct report write down Jack Ruby. They won't call."

"Is Jack Ruby someone you know? Or a made-up name?"

"I sort of knew him. He's dead now."

"Sorry."

"Don't be. Anyway, the name is beside the point. They will not call. Anyone. Who are your references?"

She looked around to make sure her interviewer wasn't coming to get her.

"They want three, but I only have one."

I took a business card out of my wallet and handed it to her.

"Use me. We met at a *Media Times* conference. You were doing an article for your college newspaper. I was impressed with your questions so I gave you a chance to write a freelance white paper for *World* Magazine."

She smiled incredulously.

"What was the paper on?"

"New media. The ways in which digital tech will impact content creation. If they ask you to forward a copy, call me and I'll send it to you."

"You're serious?"

"Absolutely. Happy to help. For your third reference, put down John Steffans—S-T-E-F-F-A-N-S—VP of Corporate Marketing. I'll give him a heads-up. If they call him—which they won't—he'll say you temped for two weeks and blew him away with your smarts."

She was speechless. Sarah Monk, having made me wait for the HR-standard, current-employee duration, came around a corner and headed my way with the fake smile she had perfected over two decades at the company.

"Paul, so good to see you. Thanks for coming down."

I never got the young woman's name but she smiled gratefully as I nodded and followed Sarah to her office. The standard small talk ensued as we walked. "Watch out for that box, Paul. That shouldn't be there. We are just sooooo busy right now with the new benefits handbooks."

Her office was similar to mine, with a large window behind her desk. In the distance, the trees of Bryant Park swayed as a summer breeze picked up. Her desk was spotless: the few manila folders that weren't locked away were stacked neatly to the right of her mouse. Her computer screen was turned so we could both see it—a bit of fake corporate transparency—but as she closed out of her web browser, a pop-up ad for a teeth-whitening product expanded to full-screen. She fumbled to close it.

"God, I hate these. And they make no sense. Why would I need this?"

She turned toward me and my eyes went straight to her teeth. They were white like white probably looks in Heaven. Her sensible blond updo and pearl necklace made her look like the governor of a Midwest state. She folded her hands on her desk.

"So Paul, how are you doing?"

"I'm OK. I mean, I'm already putting what happened upstate in perspective and I think I can get it behind me."

She nodded robotically, like a public-access talk show host lining up her next question.

"Everybody has a hard time of it now and again."

My Blackberry vibrated. I had begun to lose hope that Lamont would ever respond, but I wanted to check.

"I'm sorry, Sarah, but do you mind if I check this email for just a sec? Our Detroit rep is dealing with a Lincoln crisis."

"Of course."

She seemed to study my bandaged right hand as I reached into my breast pocket, as if she were mentally reviewing an HR training-manual chapter entitled "What to Do when an Unstable Employee Points a Handgun at You." I regretted instantly that I hadn't had the foresight to bring a water pistol to the meeting.

Lamont had responded.

Sit tight. Story breaking on Tribune.com within the hour. Not quite what you're expecting. —LL

I squeezed the Blackberry tightly with both hands.

Not quite what I'm expecting? What does that mean? Wait a minute. Oh fuck. The story is going to be about me. His side glances at Morton's were exactly what I thought they were. He figured out what Keith and I were up to that day—maybe right after Keith dropped his Red Man and I picked it up. He saw my face, he did some digging, and he found out who I am. That has to be it.

"Shit," I said.

Sarah stiffened and glared as if I had said fuck.

"Is everything alright?" she asked sternly.

"I'm sorry. Yes, it's fine. Just a complaint from Lincoln about how their ad performed in the launch issue. But we can spin our way out of it."

"OK, well don't, um, get too worked up over it. I'm sure someone on your team can handle it while you're out. Mitch did say that you would want to take a few days."

"Yes, yes. Of course."

I could hardly concentrate. I just wanted to get things over with. She opened my file, pulled out a flyer and passed it across.

"You're a valued employee, Paul. We want to make sure you avail yourself of the company's generous Employee Behavioral Health Plan. There's no cost to you. It provides five free in-person visits to a licensed network clinician and—"

"So I have to pay after five visits, right?"

"Well, yes. If you were to wish to continue, you would pay your therapist's current rate from there on in."

"Got it. Very generous."

Happy screams and shouts erupted from a group of women outside Sarah's office.

"Oh my God! Oh my God!"

"Congratulations!"

"Finally!"

"Let me see the ring!"

Sarah stood up.

"Read through the whole thing, Paul. I'll be right back to answer all your questions. OK?"

"OK."

My file remained open on her desk. Facing away from me on one side was what I recognized as my salary history. On the opposite side, affixed to the folder with a gold paper clip, was what looked like the printout of an email correspondence. I leaned back in my chair to listen to the hallway chatter. Sarah had just congratulated the bride-to-be and asked the group of women to kindly move their conversation farther down the hall. I stood up, leaned over the folder, and contorted my neck to read the back-and-forth. The subject line read *P. Cavanaugh* and the most recent message was from Mitch to Sarah:

Do Carlyle Nash a favor. Don't throw this guy away. He's the best in the biz at what he does. Regards, Mitch

I tried to read further down, but I heard Sarah saying, "I'm so happy for you" as she headed back toward her office. I picked up the behavioral health flyer and sat back down. Had Mitch really said I was *the best in the biz*? Sarah returned.

"Sorry about that, Paul. Exciting news for one of the ladies."

"Yes, I heard. That's wonderful. So, I don't really have any questions on this, but I'll certainly take advantage of the benefit. And I appreciate the short leave. I'm sure it will help. I could definitely use a breather."

I stood up.

"Wait Paul. There is just one more thing."

I sat back down.

"Yes?"

"Just so you know, I'm about to ask you a question that has been asked of every person on the *World* staff. You're not being singled out."

"OK."

"An item went missing from Mary Ellen Tanner's desk a few weeks ago. Do you know Mary Ellen?"

My heart began pounding.

"Yes. But not very well."

"Do you ever have occasion to go by her desk?"

I thought about the hallway security camera I'd spotted on the way back from her office. They would have seen me if they had viewed the footage. But, again, I could deny the theft—because I had stuffed the beach ball down my pants.

"Maybe a few times in the past year. I've gone to check on a vendor invoice here and there."

"Yes. OK. Well...that would make sense."

"Can I ask what went missing from her desk?"

"A personal effect...a Tiffany letter opener."

I felt a wave of relief.

"Wow," I said. "I thought it was going to be something important."

She looked offended as she clutched her pearls.

"Well, to some people..."

I stood up.

"Listen, I have to go deal with the Lincoln thing. Thanks for this. And no, I have no idea who took her letter opener."

"It was a *diamond* letter opener."

"Diamond? What is she, married to a Moreland or something?"

I backed out and hustled to the elevator.

* * * *

WHEN I RETURNED TO MY OFFICE, John was sitting at my computer.

"Can you fucking believe it?" he asked.

"What? What?"

He pointed to the screen. He was on the *Tribune.com* site. I raced around the desk. Executive headshots of Mitch and Simon sat side-by-side in the center of the article below a headshot of another exec I didn't recognize. The headline read:

LOU LAMONT EXCLUSIVE
Mack Howell Out at Jessup & Greer
Mitch Blake Named New CEO
Runner-Up Simon Bell Out at Carlyle Nash

"Let's go," said John.

* * * *

IT TOOK THREE DRINKS at the Millennium bar to work through every single facet of what had happened and why. In a nutshell, Mitch and Simon had both been secretly interviewing for the J&G CEO spot, probably ever since they heard J&G intended to replace Mack Howell, which would have been right around the time Mitch locked in his premiere-issue paging record. According to Lou Lamont's report, both candidates had been asked to provide consultative opinions on J&G's then-prospective acquisition of the Schrank Enthusiast Group as part of the interviewing process. Mitch's analysis clinched the job; Simon's fell just short. The problem: the Morelands had been interested in acquiring Schrank too. Neither man's betrayal—offering advice to a Carlyle Nash competitor—would be forgiven. Lawsuits and settlements would follow.

Everything made sense now with regard to the beach ball too. Mitch wanted it because he didn't need a public relations snafu, big or small, to complicate his negotiations with J&G. Simon wanted it because he'd learned Mitch was looking for it and assumed, rightly, that if Mitch wanted the ridiculous little toy that badly, there must be something about it that he could use to hurt Mitch and help himself. I told John all about my Morton's stunt with Keith and he laughed for at least 10 straight minutes. I wondered why Lamont didn't find a way to work the beach-ball story into his article, but John thought he knew. Mitch had probably leaked the bombshell news to Lamont in exchange for spiking the beach-ball story. And Lamont wouldn't want to make an enemy of Mitch now. If he did, his sources at J&G might dry up completely when Mitch took over. He had a column to fill twice a week... and Mitch would no doubt keep the steaks coming too.

Lamont sent one more email to the Savage while John and I were at the bar. He still wanted to meet, he said, just to satisfy his curiosity. But I didn't see the point. I told him I'd be in touch some future day... maybe after I got laid off. On that front, John and I didn't know what to expect. We would each have a new boss soon enough. Maybe we'd survive, maybe we wouldn't. I didn't much care.

I stepped outside to call Diane. We had talked about the madness of Carlyle Nash for so many years that I just had to tell her the big news. She was surprised by both the bombshell and my call. I told her I had made the appointment with the therapist and had met with HR about the employee assistance program. She was glad.

"When's your appointment?"

"Thursday."

"Why don't you come over for lunch on Saturday?"

"Great," I said. "I'll be there."

She asked me about a section of the electric bill that didn't make sense to her. As I tried to explain, I saw Jennie emerge from the parking garage across 44th Street. She smiled and waved, but I could tell even from afar that the news had shaken her. I smiled and waved back.

"You know what, Diane? Just send it to my work fax. I'll figure it out."

Jennie approached as I ended the call.

She was a bit breathless.

"Unbelievable news," she said. "Are you OK?"

"I guess so. Are you OK?"

She bowed her head and began to cry.

"I don't know. I just..."

I hugged her for a while. We skipped the movie. ▪

CHAPTER TWENTY-FIVE

World Ends

(2008)

ANOTHER THING MY FATHER and I agreed upon was how annoying it is when you go to someone's house and the first thing they want to do is give you a tour: *This room used to be an office, but once the boys outgrew the bunk beds we decided to take down the wall that was here. You remember that wall, right? No? Come on. The wall...that was right here?*

As my father would say during the ride home, *Please...just offer me a drink, set out a bowl of chips, and ask me how I'm doing— because I don't give a shit about your crown molding.*

I feel the same way about talking about therapy. I could go on and on about the dark places I went to in six months of sessions, but it would be way too boring. What I will say is that it was one of the best experiences of my life. Sometimes the only thing we need is for someone to replace the dead light bulbs in those pitch-black corners. But maybe the best endorsement I can offer is that after about three months, people stopped telling me how tired I looked.

Another thing happened at the three-month mark: I went

back to slinging hash. OK, that's not true. It's one thing to pick up a sausage-and-egg for Keith; it's another to make it for him. That I didn't do. We usually had our breakfast sandwiches delivered.

It was Diane's idea that I sign a one-year lease on the old apartment, to give myself time to focus solely on what makes me tick. We agreed I would see her and Aidan regularly, but neither of us wanted to rush the repairs we were trying to make to our relationship. We wanted them to be successful—solid and lasting—and that would take time and patience. It's just funny that as I was learning more about myself, I learned a lot about Keith too—that he was lactose intolerant, for one thing, and that his favorite animal is the mountain lion.

Finally, one *more* thing that happened at the three-month mark: I went to work for John at Carlyle Nash Corporate. The company elevated Simon's second-in-command, Christopher Hart, to head the group. Hart was a low-wattage choice to replace Simon, but that's what the Morelands wanted. They were done, it seemed, with big personalities and profligate spenders. That they might be ushering in an era of boredom and contraction seemed lost on them. Luckily for John, he had a good relationship with Hart. He talked me up as digitally savvy—a lie—and before long I was shifted over from the rudderless, Thad-led *World*. It was for significantly less than Simon had offered, but a lateral move was fine with me. Word had it that the Morelands were planning to shutter *World*. Two issues later they did just that. As reported by Lou Lamont, the multimillion-dollar enterprise fell victim to a contracting economy, editorial dysfunction under Jimmy Stillman, and poor business leadership after Mitch's departure. The article was headlined "From Thunk To Thud," but Lamont made a point of reminding readers that *World* had debuted to "record-breaking ad-side success under Blake's strong leadership." He was probably cutting into a ribeye at Morton's as the story hit.

It was fairly amazing to me that I hung on at Carlyle Nash. I thought my meltdown would follow me around forever, but it didn't, probably because most Carlyle Nashers are too focused on themselves—how they fit, where they're headed, what their boss thinks of them—to care much about what happens to anyone else.

I finally knew what Mitch thought of me, though: *the best in the biz at what he does.* Those words may very well have saved my job. And then he was gone. Just like that. Naomi packed up his things and had them shipped to J&G the day the news broke. As conflicted as I felt, I sent him an email a week later to thank him for everything. He responded immediately, telling me how much he appreciated my work, my sacrifices and, yes, my loyalty. He didn't mention my meltdown. Someone else might have interpreted that as a sign of his willingness to look past it. However, I knew that wasn't the case. The minute I had pushed those printouts to the center of the table at the offsite, my time in Mitch Blake's inner circle had ended. I might have felt otherwise if he had come out to the curb to check on me that day. But he hadn't; he'd gone on with the meeting. I suppose a part of me will always hold that against him. If something like that had happened when I worked for Leo Breslin, my old deli manager, he would have been hot on my heels. He would have lifted me to my feet, offered me a smoke, and asked, "What the fuck was that all about back there?"

Then again, maybe I had always expected too much of Mitch. My therapist once asked me to consider the possibility that I was just as emotionally inscrutable as he was. She posited that perhaps as I delivered one buttoned-up project after another, I had lulled him into thinking that I was able to separate work from life as efficiently as he did—that I also operated unfailingly at the press of a button. So when he pressed the button at Mohonk and my hard drive froze, all he could think to do was switch to a laptop and wait until I rebooted. Finally, my therapist asked a question I'm not sure I'll ever be able to answer:

"Would *you* have followed you out?" Maybe I just don't want to answer that one.

Around the time of my sixth month in therapy, John and I were returning from what we called a "moderation" lunch: typically a steak and one glass of wine with a generous pour—OK, fine, two glasses—when a familiar face passed us in the lobby. It took me a few seconds to place her, so by the time I remembered that I owed her an apology she was already revolving out to the street. It was the tarot card lady. I supposed she had stopped by to confirm another gig for one of the brands. When you're accurate, positive word of mouth follows.

John and I chatted about a project on our way up in the elevator, but all I could think about was the last card the tarot lady had flipped over during my reading: the one of the man with swords sticking out of his body. It wasn't that I hadn't thought of that card before; I had just never felt ready to investigate the meaning of the foreboding image. *Would I be fired by forty? Divorced by fifty? Dead by sixty?*

When I returned to my office—an interior one right across from John's—I closed the door and googled "tarot card swords in back." I found it right away: the Ten of Swords. A man is lying face down on the ground. Ten swords are plunged deep in his back from his neck to his thighs. A vast body of water and a mountainous landscape are on the horizon. The sky above is black with clouds, but a golden sunrise illuminates a strip of yellow sky beneath them.

For the next hour, I read through different analyses of the meaning of the card. The prevailing interpretation was one of "bottoming out." If you draw the Ten of Swords, you stand on the brink of a sudden failure or disaster that you cannot prevent. However, once you absorb the often self-inflicted hit and the aftershocks of self-pity, dawn arrives and spiritual rejuvenation follows.

I printed out one of the images, glued it to an index card, and pinned it to my bulletin board—far enough behind my computer monitor that only I could see it. The only time I take it down now is when I have to give a presentation. I set my index cards on the podium with the Ten of Swords card on top. When I look down at it, I don't see a man lying on the ground with swords in his back. I see a middle manager sitting on a curb crying only for himself.

Then I raise my head, smile, and search for a friendly face. ▪

Donuts and Dust

(A Few Years Later)

JENNIE WANTED A DESTINATION wedding in the Bahamas. On the beach. She said she felt closer to God near the ocean. I'm partial to old churches and burning incense, but as I watched her walk down the sandy aisle— barefoot and ethereal—I reconsidered. Maybe she was right.

Getting a babysitter for the long weekend had proved impossible, so Jennie and Bob had insisted that Diane and I bring the kids. It said a lot about the type of person she is, and the kind of guy she was marrying. Bob was a keeper—and he had grown up just a town over from me. Slung hash back in the day himself.

My mother would have happily taken the kids, but she had passed two years earlier, and Diane and I agreed it wouldn't be fair to ask any of our siblings to take them. It's not that Aidan is a handful. In fact, he has grown into a surprisingly easygoing little boy. The twins, however, are a nightmare: toddlers with hair-trigger tempers. And our only other babysitting options were one-night-only teens.

The truth, though, was that Diane and I were happy to have the kids along. Me especially. After my mother passed, we didn't want to put them in daycare right away. Diane was up for a promotion at the hospital, so I transitioned to a work-at-home contract role. It was for less money, but it shielded me from the endless layoffs that plagued Carlyle Nash in the post-Mitch/ Simon years. With at-home work came full-time parenting, which I discovered I loved. In some cosmic tradeoff I may never fully understand, I turned into the perpetually patient counter-balance to not just one, but two screaming ids.

Sadly for others, I'm now that parent in a restaurant who looks like he's not doing enough to control his children. But it's not for lack of trying. The twins are built to a code not soon broken. In fact, I think all humans are just wired a certain way, and they need time to master their unique circuitries. More and more, I see my task as just staying calm for the kids' sake. And for my sake. I'm also learning that I'll probably never be able to control anyone anyway, especially the kids. But really, what the hell do I know? I'm still a savage.

Speaking of which, I do run into Emily on occasion—typical-ly when I'm back in the building to meet with Corporate about some project. We chat, but the conversations are shorter each time. We probably make better adversaries than lovers anyway. She thinks having children is mundane. It doesn't surprise me.

We were all out on the beach the morning after the wedding when Diane decided to go for a run. As I sat in the low tide watching Aidan splash in front of me with Caroline propped on one leg and James on the other, she leaned down and kissed me goodbye. Her damp auburn ringlets cooled my bare shoulders.

"You do know that I'm the best thing that ever happened to you, right?" she asked.

"Without a doubt," I said, blinking up at her in the bright morning sun.

Aidan was venturing further out into the foaming surf, un-afraid but aware, stopping when the water was just above his waist. I watched him steel his little body against the waves, rev-eling in the rush and testing his limits. I tried to imagine his future and hoped that he, like me, would have the chance to test his limits in the world and would come through it intact, with perspective, and at peace. I prayed that I'd be around long enough to watch for a while.

Caroline leaned over and tried to bite James, which started him wailing, so I planted them on opposite sides of the beach blanket. Aidan ran up and dripped all over Caroline. She started crying too. I threw Aidan a towel and tried to find the twins' pacifiers in one of the jam-packed totes we had dragged down to the beach with us. Diane and I had become less and less organized of late. I suppose a certain sense of contentment can do that. I waded through books, bibs, snacks, sippy cups, a corkscrew, toys, iPhone chargers, a magnifying glass, a check register, and more in my fruitless search for the "binkies." By the time I gave up, the twins had stopped crying. Aidan had given each of them a mini donut to gnaw on instead.

"Nice work, my boy." I said.

"They love donuts, Daddy."

"Everyone loves donuts, Buddy."

Watching Aidan munch on his own donut, I suddenly felt bad that, when Diane and I are gone from this world, he and the twins will have to sort through all the crap we've amassed. I made a mental note that it was time for Diane and me to get things in order. Then again, you can learn an awful lot about a parent when it comes time to go through their possessions. I have my mother's handwritten crime novel to prove it. Wall-to-wall sex and violence. I guess nine kids will do that to you.

I'm not sure what my children will learn about me when I go off to take my lumps from Dad and Uncle Frank, but I do know some of the things they'll come across in our attic. For one thing, there's a large plastic bin just to the right of the central air-conditioning unit we had Keith install for us. It holds hundreds of work samples tracing my career from its beginnings at *Blowback* to the heights of *Bellwether* to my brief but eventful time at *World*. It's all pretty useless: the yellowing editorial clips, the glossy saddle-stitched presentations, and the turnaround papers for Mitch. But they might enjoy going through it.

The beach ball is in there too.

If Diane is also gone by then, they might puzzle over the beach ball for a while. I imagine them all grown up, sitting amid the dust of the attic and the mists of my life, wondering what it's doing there...and why I kept it. Or maybe they won't.

Maybe they'll toss it aside and move on to my custom-framed college diploma. They may find that more meaningful...but I hope they don't examine it too closely.

They just might figure out it's fake. ▪

Acknowledgments

I CAN'T SAY I EVER MET BRENDAN GILL, who wrote for *The New Yorker* from 1936 until his death in 1997, but he made an impact on me. Two years before his passing, he published his final book—a copy of which sat atop a stack in my first cubicle at the magazine. As a technician installed my phone, I picked up *Late Bloomers*. In it, Gill explored an intriguing archetype: the person whose most notable achievements come later in life, or, as he wrote, people who "succeeded in finding themselves." In the book's foreword, he added: "To find oneself is plainly to have been lost. It is to have been stumbling about in a dark wood and to have encountered there, unexpectedly and yet how welcomely, a second self, capable of leading one out into the safety of a sunny upland meadow."

I was 29 when I first read that sentence, and I hadn't yet entered my own dark wood. Soon enough, like many in the media life, I would. But just as Mr. Gill described, a second self would indeed pull me out into the sunlight two decades later...holding a manuscript. And while this novel won't win a Pulitzer, it is certainly my most notable creative achievement to date. Many thanks, dear reader, for picking it up.

On to the rest of my thank-yous...

First and foremost to Maricel, my beautiful wife, who treats every person she meets the same way: with kindness, grace, and good humor. You are the best person I've ever known and the best editor I never knew I had. And of course to our children:

the compassionate and creative Conor, the joyfully quick-witted Patrick, and Cristina, dauntless little force of nature. You are gifts from God, and my love for you knows no bounds.

To Greenpoint Press and the publishing team to which I am indebted: the great Charles Salzberg; designer extraordinaire Bob Lascaro; and my editor, Gini Kopecky Wallace, who performed small miracles on page after page. My deepest thanks to each of you for believing in this novel and for your considerable investments in it.

To *Ducts*, the online magazine that encouraged me since publishing my very first short humor piece, and shocked me by republishing it in their *Best of Ducts* anthology. Special thanks to founder Jonathan Kravetz, former humor editor Dan McCoy, and—the best thing about working with *Ducts*—my talented friend Gail Eisenberg. Stay in the chair, motherfucker.

This book would not and could not exist without Matt Roberts—my great friend and provider of vital feedback. I never should have stabbed you in the back, Matt. But I'd probably do it again.

And to my equally great friend and mentor, Michael Kane. Thanks for 20 years of laughs, sound advice, and lunches that are never long enough.

To many more industry friends, memorable colleagues, and valued mentors or teachers through the years, all of whom are important to this book and/or my career in ways they may not know: Andrea Abbott, Dawn Akins, Doug Bachelis, Melinda Barlow, Richard Beckman, David Carey, Angi Collins, Pastor Rodney Eberhardt, Thomas Frosch, Theresa Gaffney, Jim Heidt, Marty Kahnle, Jane Kaupp, Stuart Keating, Kari Kovach, Babette Lazarus, Mitch Levenberg, Tim Lempke, James Oates, Steven Pressfield, Roselle Schjong, Daniella Wells, and Marie Wolpert. Plus special nods to Gwen Cooper, a great writer who has no idea how much she inspired me, and to Tom Rock, eminent co-author of the *Top Ten Things Never Said at Division Avenue Deli*. My thanks to you both for the killer blurbs.

A lifetime of thanks...

To Bill Henry and Chris Gibbons, my best friends since second grade, for decades of laughter and inspiration with the brothers we picked up along the way: Jerry Farina, Chris Haag, Rich Hellberg, Rob Koscik, and Ed Wahl.

To my beloved siblings and their wonderful spouses: Patty, Dennis, John, Bill, George, Jim, Margaret, and respectively Murph, Noreen, Elly, Camille, Brenda, Leah, and Mark. I'm grateful to know you as both family and friends. (And if you buy copies in bulk, I promise to have Christmas at my house this year.) Thanks also to my late in-laws, Oscar and Elsa Peón, who are greatly missed, and to my brother-in-law, Carlos, a great guy.

To my late Uncle Robert O'Connor for filling our world with endless laughter, and to my dear departed Uncle Bill O'Connor for "Paul MacTavish" and *Zero Night Punch*. But even bigger thanks to my Uncle John O'Connor for his encouragement and hard-won wisdom from the media trenches.

To my mother, Mary Farrell. The funniest O'Connor of them all. I love you, Mom, and I owe you the world. But if you don't take down that sign in my old room, we're finished.

And, finally, to my late father, George Farrell, a great writer and a gentle soul. Thanks for the visit, Pop. I did what you told me. ·

About the Author

GERARD FARRELL has worked in the magazine industry since the late '90s for brands including *The New Yorker*, *Rolling Stone*, *Allure*, and the ill-fated business magazine *Condé Nast Portfolio*. His short humor has appeared in the literary anthology *The Man Who Ate His Book*, and he is a frequent contributor to the literary  webzine *Ducts*. He is currently working on his second novel, *Tailspin*, the story of a disgraced salesman seeking revenge on the temp who got him fired.

He lives in Farmingdale, NY with his wife, Maricel, their children Conor, Patrick, and Cristina, and Holly the Cat.

To learn more visit: ggfarrell.com

CPSIA information can be obtained
at www.ICGtesting.com
Printed in the USA
BVHW03s1912220618
519803BV00001B/7/P

9 780990 619475